I COULD BE MUTE

The Life and Work of Gladys Schmitt

Edited by
Anita Brostoff

Carnegie Series in English
Gerald Costanzo, General Editor
New Series—Number One
Carnegie-Mellon University
Pittsburgh 1978

Publication of this volume has been made possible by a grant from the Wherrett Memorial
Fund of the Pittsburgh Foundation.

I COULD BE MUTE

The Life and Work of Gladys Schmitt

Edited by
Anita Brostoff

Carnegie-Mellon University Press
Pittsburgh and London 1978

The sonnets quoted on pages 50, 100, 129, and the page facing the copyright page are from *Sonnets for an Analyst* by Gladys Schmitt, copyright © 1973 by the Estate of Gladys Schmitt. Reprinted by permission of Harcourt Brace Jovanovich, Inc.

Library of Congress Catalog Card Number: 78-59831
ISBN 0-915604-21-3 (cloth)
ISBN 0-915604-22-1 (pbk.)
ISSN 0069-0678 Carnegie Series in English
Copyright © 1978 by Anita Brostoff
Printed and bound in the United States of America
First Edition

I could refuse to answer. Like the snow,
Silence could mound me round and dignify
The shale-sharp anger and the ragweed lie,
The bones, the seeds, what rots, what still might grow—
But not at zero or at ten below.
Taking my coloring from the vacant sky,
I could lie blank until the day I die,
And you could always ask and never know.
I could be mute and strike one sparrow blind,
Keep him too dazed to fly away or light,
Hold him still fluttering over vapid white,
Baffle and craze him with that woman's mind,
That woman's soul, that spurious mystery
Which all men want and no man ever had of me.

Sonnets for an Analyst

PREFACE

This book was originally conceived because its authors believe Gladys Schmitt has not gained the recognition she deserves as a writer. In building our essays, we hoped to arouse interest in her as a woman as well as to bring attention to her novels and poems. While this stance gave us a common starting point, we never quite expected that our separate responses to and interpretations of Schmitt's life and work would agree as they have, would create such a consistent portrait and appraisal. We present this portrait and appraisal with the hope that it will prompt further study of Gladys Schmitt— teacher, writer, woman.

My thanks first and foremost are to my friend and colleague Lois Josephs Fowler, without whose ideas and constant guidance this book would never have existed.

I am most grateful to the A.W. Mellon Educational and Charitable Trust, which provided the basic financial support for publication of the book, and to its Director, Theodore Hazlett. I thank also the Maurice R. Robinson Fund and the English Department of Carnegie-Mellon University for additional funds and help in publication.

I am greatly indebted to Gerald Costanzo, Director of Carnegie-Mellon University Press, who reviewed, helped revise, and finally approved the manuscript for publication. Erwin R. Steinberg read the manuscript, suggested revisions, and provided helpful guidance throughout its history. Jan Cohn also reviewed the manuscript and made suggestions for revision. Elizabeth Culley designed the cover for this volume and helped me in countless other ways. I thank Anne Skoog of Hunt Library, Carnegie-Mellon University, for her help in the researching of Schmitt's life and especially for access to the photographs reproduced in this book. I owe special thanks to M. R. Robinson, who gave me important information about some of the dates and facts of Schmitt's life, and who has been most gracious to me. I thank Karen Seles, who typed and retyped parts of the manuscript. And I thank Harcourt Brace Jovanovich for permission to print four of Schmitt's *Sonnets for an Analyst,* and Elizabeth Culley for permission to print Schmitt's "Consider the Giraffe."

Finally, I am deeply grateful to my husband, Philip, and my children, whose patience gave me the time and whose support gave me the nourishment to do the research, writing, editing, and communicating I have done in helping to create this book.

Anita Brostoff

Carnegie-Mellon University
May, 1978

CONTENTS

INTRODUCTION

The questions asked in this book about Gladys Schmitt's life and work are important questions for women, because the issues involved provoke us, threaten us. Basically, the questions come down to this: how is it that a woman of extraordinary intellectual power and remarkable artistic talent, who published nine novels and many short stories and poems, never gained a substantial and sustained reputation as a writer, either with the literary world or with the reading public; and how is it that a woman who possessed vibrant warmth and humor and charm, who was the center around which swarmed—like bees to honey—loving friends and adoring students, who was heaped with awards and honors for her writing and teaching, who inspired immeasurable respect and devotion from those who knew her, could find no permanence in any gratification and remained all her life seriously and fundamentally unfulfilled?

The authors of this book, women who knew and worked with Gladys Schmitt, have immersed ourselves in the various aspects of her life and works, exploring these two questions. We have remembered, re-read, re-synthesized thought and feeling. The speaker of the sonnet ("I could refuse to answer"), through the words and acts we remember, and through the words she wrote, has herself helped to unlock the mystery of her woman's mind, her woman's soul. And although our readers will find here and there differing interpretations of her life or her work, overall they will find, I believe, a remarkable convergence of our separate ideas, a coherence which finally expresses the whole person and reveals the paradox of her success and failure.

I want to consider first here what I take to be the less crucial of the two questions: her uncertain reputation as a writer. I did not mean to imply, above, that the critics ignored her. Indeed, her praises were sung by Important Men: Roger Sale, Gilbert Highet, Louis Untermeyer, Clifton Fadiman, Orville Prescott, Stanley Edgar Hyman, Lionel Trilling—this is not a roster to be taken lightly. And the praise was generous: reviews of her first novel, *The Gates of Aulis*, hailed her as a genius; Whit Burnett called her "the American Proust"; Hiram Haydn said of *Rembrandt* that it stood beside

Tolstoy's majestic novels. The critics granted that here was a mind that grappled with grand themes, here was a *talent* to be reckoned with.

Why, then, we ask, did they not do so? Only Edmund Fuller attempted to examine the body of her work—and this only partially (the big "historical" novels *David the King, Confessors of the Name,* and *Rembrandt*), with apologies to the novels with "modern" settings, which he put aside. Only Hadyn reflected on the puzzle— why her oeuvre has been thus neglected:

> I don't understand, whether in terms of . . . Gladys Schmitt, or others who seem to me among our best novelists. I tell myself that they were born at the wrong time, that current literary fashions, the predilections of the governing elite and the luck of the game are the contributing factors to their relative obscurity—or at least to their seldom receiving what I believe their just recognition. But I don't really know, and it's a question that plagues me past tolerance.[1]

Like Hadyn, we don't really know; but we have some ideas.

Peggy Knapp, in discussing Schmitt's character and early writing, up to and including *Aulis,* directs us to Schmitt's fault of excessiveness. Almost all the critics agreed on this point, even while they praised her. And it may be that they, and the reading public as well, mentally wrote her off long before she learned to overcome this trait in her writing, since in one way or another there was too much —words, passion, psychology, or philosophy—for most stomachs in every one of the big novels before *Electra.* Writing personality aside, Jan Cohn goes to the heart of the problem when she describes the disjunction between the historical fiction form, a genre now reserved for popular entertainment, and the high seriousness of Schmitt's psychologic, moral, and philosophic concerns. Way back in 1961, Fuller saw this unusual marriage of form and substance as a reason for the critical slight to her work and admonished his fellows to take note:

> There is a tendency among our critics to overlook or deprecate what we are forced by prevailing usage to call "historical," "biblical" or "biographical" novels. Because much shoddy stuff or merely competent hack work is so labeled, it takes the reputation of a Thomas Mann or a Sholem Asch to persuade some people of the literary respectability of the forms. Gladys Schmitt, working in all three categories with her illuminating way of seeing the past, demonstrates that we should not allow a hyphenation of the novel to obscure our view of what a gifted artist can achieve in any variety of this protean medium.[2]

Fuller was right, but that didn't either sell books to the public or convince critics to take more serious notice.

The second question, what happened to Schmitt herself, concerns us even more than what has happened to her books. Pursuing this topic, we have recounted her life experience: Betty Culley, her niece and adopted daughter, takes an overall view of her life, remembering the quirks of the Schmitt family, Gladys' dominant role in it, and her often stormy relationships with the others; Sarah Strauss, Gladys' lifelong friend, tells from a confidante's point of view some of Gladys' experiences in and beyond the confines of the family; Lois Fowler, who knew Gladys and her husband Simon Goldfield in their later years, examines the emotional effects of a frustrated marriage where male and female roles were symbiotically reversed. We have looked also at Gladys' creative achievements, not only in writing fiction and poetry but also in teaching and in needlework. Her friend Dorothy Rosenberg talks about the needle-work and the part it played in Gladys' emotional life. Barbara Beyer, a graduate student who studied with Gladys, and herself a teacher, shows us Gladys in an actual taped class session.

All of us see Gladys Schmitt as a woman of prodigious ability and accomplishment, but as a woman driven, angry, guilty, fearful, self-denigrating, anguished. Not that she didn't have joy of her work and of the recognition and rewards she did receive, and not that she didn't appreciate the everyday pleasures of her life—the beauty of her home, the closeness of friends and relatives, the parties she gave, even the good clothes she wore—but that there were deep psychic failures. Two themes, two explanations for these failures, emerge most insistently from our writing: first, Schmitt's sense of inadequacy as a woman and her striving to compensate for this felt inadequacy—her striving to accept herself and to be accepted and loved as a woman; and second, her perceived failure to win this struggle, with the resulting exhaustion, compromise, and ironic resignation.

Searching for the causes and effects of this struggle in Gladys Schmitt, we have centered on her continual inability to resolve her role problems. We have found that she was strongly socialized to be feminine; yet she felt she was physically unattractive and inept at domestic tasks. Early religious training ingrained in her the necessity to feel and act out of compassion—a feminine as well as a Christian virtue; yet her strong drive for self-fulfillment made her feel constant guilt and conflict. In her adult years she functioned as

13

a male, as teacher, writer, even breadwinner; but she had an in-ordinate fear of independence and imposed severe constraints on her own freedom. She felt thwarted on all fronts: she wanted to write tragedy in the novel, she said in a 1933 diary entry, but could not "Because I am a woman, I am defeated, and could not write a tragedy if a second Hamlet died under my very nose—any more than I could make (without spilling things all over the kitchen) a pot of tea." (One motive for writing novels set in the past, when tragedy, she thought, was more possible than it is today, was surely to reach this goal.) In her need to be loved, she gave of her time and vitality to the point of sacrifice and worked herself well beyond her physical capacity—excessive in this as in so many other ways. Still, this giving wasn't enough; and if, as she thought, she couldn't be loved for her feminine beauty, and she couldn't be loved for her noble actions, she hoped to be accepted and loved for these qualities in her writing. When she was twenty-five and working on *Aulis,* she wrote this in a letter:

> In the life of the world it is necessary to be, a great deal of the time, slipshod, slippery, hypocritical, silent when you should be using your tongue for justice, without courage, awkward, unlovely, com-promising, afraid. I am all these things by day and night . . . . But in that hour and a half when I write what I choose, what I know, what I believe to the bottom of my soul, even to the bottom of the bone and flesh which holds the mind—then I am good and whole and sure in my own eyes. This is a blessedness. I feel that all that I was during the day I am now no more. Am I ugly? My sentences are beautiful. Did I compromise? Here there is no compromise. Was I wavering and afraid? Here I walk surely. Have I whimpered and been cheap? In this work of mine I am given back my silence and my dignity.

In fact, Schmitt's writing clearly reflects her role problems. In my own essay in this book I have examined her major heroines, to find that in every case, their sexuality is at stake; the fertility, the re-generative power of the female is what they are all after. Lois Lamdin's essay on *Sonnets for an Analyst* shows how Schmitt in her later years openly confessed her lifelong struggle, forcing herself to confine and thus control the anguish of reliving it through the tight structure of the sonnet form. The *Sonnets*—they are fine, really not to be missed—show too in what ways Schmitt came to terms with herself and her role at last, and with what enormous and moving suffering. And Pamela McCorduck describes how the young Schmitt created a heroine (in *Aulis*) who battles to become a whole woman, balanced between the extremes of self-abnegation and self-fulfillment, while the old, sick Schmitt created a heroine (in *The God-forgotten*) who accepts in resignation a self-abnegating role. McCorduck asserts that at the end of her life Schmitt tragically yielded, out of spiritual fatigue, to an impoverished concept of woman.

If Schmitt had such pervasive difficulties with her femininity, we ask also whether her feminine socialization might have hindered the flowering of her talent. There would have been in her psyche, however muted, the historical attitude that women should be modest and chaste—that is, not famous; and as Virginia Woolf remarked in *A Room of One's Own,* this attitude is certainly hostile to the state of mind needed to write. And why did Schmitt work in the midst of her noisy household? Surely such a strong-willed woman, who bought the house they lived in and was earning the food everybody ate, could have demanded some peace and quiet, a place to concentrate—a corner, if not a room, of her own! Would shutting herself away from her family have made her feel too guilty? Furthermore, and perhaps most damaging of all to her writing, there is the fact that she often wrote subjectively. Schmitt understood all along the limiting effect, the dangers, of such a practice. In her 1933 diary (before *Aulis*), she quoted Leonardo: "The painter must not paint in his own image because he, himself, may not be beautiful and therefore that which he paints will not be beautiful either." And she went on to say: "Now I remember that all the time, and it is a kind of reproach, there is nothing silly about it; perhaps it is the symbol of the difference between the scientific and the lyrical, the objective and the subjective, the intellect and the emotion. If I cannot be great it is because of that—because I draw in my own image." The lyrical, the subjective, the emotional—all, traditionally, are considered female traits. And this book shows that Schmitt continued to draw in her own image. It may be, then, that her problems and struggles as a woman trapped her finally into an intellectual bind, ironically an inability to be androgynous, to project herself completely into either sex, as a fine mind must.

It may be that Gladys Schmitt would have been a happier human being and an even greater writer if she could have escaped the effects of her socialization. It may be that she needed to be free to be what she was—a talented human being. If so, her Gestalt surely reflects the experience of other talented women who have missed a full measure of recognition and who are unable to fulfill themselves as women *or* as artists. I think this dilemma of the conflicts and confusions talented women face (even those with lesser gifts, such as we, teachers and writers, have) is what this book is finally about.

Women now are unearthing and expressing the commonality of female experience; and women are forging viable alternatives to man's world, woman's place. But they are still subject to traditional female socialization; they still suffer, if less traumatically than Gladys Schmitt, confusion and conflict about their roles; they still encounter barriers to full achievement. Therefore women need to communicate with each other—and with men, too—about what is common to them. Because Schmitt's life illuminates this common experience, and even more because her achievements as teacher and writer are great, it is important for us to communicate her experience. It is important for us to bring attention to her literary works—especially *David, Rembrandt, The Godforgotten,* and the *Sonnets*—which are the fruits of this experience. In doing so we take our cue from Schmitt herself, who understood the dimensions of her talent, understood her conflicts and failures, and spoke about them to men and women in her teaching and writing. Taking the harder and nobler way, she chose not to be mute.

Anita Brostoff

NOTES

[1]Hiram Hadyn, *Words and Faces* (New York: Harcourt Brace Jovanovich, 1965), p. 224.

[2]Edmund Fuller, "Gladys Schmitt: 'Jacob and the Angel,' " *American Scholar,* XXXI (Summer, 1961), 411.

GLADYS SCHMITT:
A CHRONOLOGY

1909   Gladys Leonore Schmitt is born on May 31 in Pittsburgh, PA to Henry H. and Leonore Elizabeth (Link) Schmitt.

1911   Her sister Dorothy is born.

1913   Her brother Bob is born.

1914   The family moves out of George and Hattie Schmitt's house. (George was Gladys' father's brother, Hattie was Gladys' mother's sister.)

1917   Gladys writes several plays in verse, four of which are staged at the elementary school she attends.

1918   She starts writing poetry.

1920   Her grandmother dies.

1921   She "loses" her God (the event described in sonnet 12, *Sonnets for an Analyst*).

1924   She writes 300 pages of a highly romantic novel, then throws it away unfinished.

1926   She meets Simon Goldfield.

1927   "John Keats," an essay, is printed in *Scholastic* (October 1). Gladys receives five dollars for the essay.

      She wins a high school *Scholastic Magazines* award (third prize) for the poem "Women." It has three sections, rhymed monologues: "Lucrezia Borzia," "Saint Joan," and "Ruth."

      She writes a second novel, *Candle Saga*, about the Danish conquest of England in 950 A.D. (This 450 page unpublished novel is now lost.)

      She graduates from Schenley High School.

      Through the *Scholastic* award, she receives a scholarship to Pennsylvania College for Women.

1928   She receives a scholarship to the University of Pittsburgh and transfers.

The University of Pittsburgh magazine, *Steps*, prints "Sister Joan" (May).

1929   She meets M. R. Robinson, publisher of *Scholastic Magazines*, at Pitt English Department parties. Later Robinson begins to "date" her.

Her first important publication, "Progeny," is in *Poetry* (September, vol. XXXIV, no. 6).

1930-31   She writes a sonnet sequence, "In a Lean Year," and the personal essay "Frere."

1931   The *Owl*, a University of Pittsburgh magazine, prints four sonnets.

She wins the Witter Bynner National College Poetry Award—first prize for a poem on Joan of Arc.

"Sister Joan" and "Song of Helen" are published in *Best College Verse*.

1932   She is elected to Phi Beta Kappa.

She graduates from Pitt, magna cum laude.

1933   She takes courses for her M.A. degree, but leaves Pitt to go to work for *Scholastic Magazines* as an assistant editor.

1933-35   She begins and throws away three novels. She completes one experimental novel, using stream of consciousness through four points of view.

1934   "House Divided" is published in the May issue of *Story*—her first published fiction.

"Saturday" is published in the June issue of *Atlantic Monthly*. She is paid $100 for the story.

Robinson is married to Florence Liddell, who works for *Scholastic*; Gladys is despondent.

Her sister Dorothy is ill (1934-1936).

Gladys is ill, and tuberculosis is suspected.

1935   The poems "Self-Defense" and "Evil Husbandry" are published in *Tone* (January, no. 4., p. 8).

Gladys is working on *The Gates of Aulis*.

18

Simon looks for a job as a private secretary.

1936 "The Cabinet," a short story, is published in *Household Magazine.*

1937 A close friend from Pitt commits suicide.

Gladys and Simon Goldfield are married on November 27. They take an apartment across the street from Gladys' family.

1939 Gladys and Simon move to New York with *Scholastic Magazines.* Gladys is promoted to Associate Editor, at $165 a month. Robinson gets Simon a job at Harper's.

1942 Gladys decides to leave *Scholastic.* Gladys and Simon return to Pittsburgh and move in with Gladys' parents.

Gladys is offered a teaching job at Carnegie Institute of Technology for $1800 a year.

The Gates of Aulis is published. She wins the Dial Press award of $1000 for a book by "an author who has not hitherto published a book of fiction."

Gladys writes "Consider the Giraffe," later (1944) published in *It's a Woman's World,* a collection of short fiction from *Harper's Bazaar.*

Simon gets a job as an inspector with the OPA (rent control authority). He is paid $2000 a year, later $200 a month.

1943 Simon is rejected from the army because of poor vision.

"All Souls" is sold to *Colliers* for $750. It is published in the November 6 issue and republished by Colliers in *Prize Stories of 1944.*

1944 Gladys is ill all year; in the fall she takes a semester's leave of absence.

Gladys' mother has a heart attack.

Simon gets a job at a government housing project.

"The Mirror," *Colliers,* May 6.

"The Mourners," *Harper's Bazaar,* May.

"The Furlough," *Mademoiselle.*

1945 *David the King* is selected by the Literary Guild.

Gladys buys the big house on Wilkins Avenue with the down payment from the Literary Guild.

Her brother Bob's daughter, Betty, comes to live with Gladys and Simon, along with Gladys' parents, her sister Dorothy, and her Aunt Ollie.

"Another Spring," *Harper's Bazaar,* February.

"The Matchmaking," *Colliers,* September.

"The Avenger," *Good Housekeeping,* December.

1946 *David the King* (Dial Press).

Gladys begins a novel about a teacher's commitment to students. She discards it and begins *Alexandra.*

"It's been a Long Time," Yearbook of *Writer's Digest.*

She sells a story to *Cosmopolitan* for $2000.

"Who Killed Goliath," *Carnegie Magazine,* May, pp. 6-7.

Simon is thinking of retiring.

Gladys' sister Dorothy has an operation and is left temporarily paralyzed. Gladys takes care of her.

1947 *Alexandra* (Dial Press).

1950 Gladys' father dies.

"The Mist and the Magic," *Today's Woman.*

1952 *Confessors of the Name* is published by Dial Press and becomes a Literary Guild selection.

1953 A friend from Pitt (female) commits suicide.

Gladys' cousin George Schmitt dies of a coronary at age 47.

Her mother has another heart attack.

Simon's mother dies.

Gladys is promoted to Professor of English at Carnegie Tech.

"I Am Exhibit A," *Carnegie Magazine,* May, pp. 194-152. This was originally a speech delivered at the *Scholastic* awards banquet, April 1.

"The Day Before the Wedding," *Good Housekeeping.*

1954 Aunt Ollie dies.

"The Uninvited," *Seventeen Magazine,* August.

"The Man Who Found Himself," *Colliers,* September 17.

1955 *The Persistent Image* (Dial Press).

1956 Gladys has angina.

1957 *A Small Fire* (Dial Press).

1959 Simon is thought to have glaucoma.

Gladys' mother dies after a long, debilitating illness, during which Gladys and the family care for her.

These two events cause Gladys a physical crackup; she can't eat and loses twelve pounds.

After eight years of not working, Simon takes a job with the Housing Authority.

Dorothy takes her own apartment, living separate from the family for the first time.

Betty is married.

Simon is translating the *Iliad*.

1960 Gladys finishes *Rembrandt*. She had filled 7,000 note cards with detailed information from her research.

1961 *Rembrandt* is published by Random House and becomes a Literary Guild selection.

Gladys is named a Distinguished Daughter of Pennsylvania.

She receives an Honorary Doctor of Letters from the University of Pittsburgh.

1962 "Is Fiction's Future in the Past?," *New York Times Book Review,* April 22.

The Heroic Deeds of Beowulf, a children's book (Random House).

Simon has an emotional breakdown (March).

Gladys has an emotional breakdown, six months after Simon's breakdown.

1962-65 While in psychoanalysis, Gladys writes *Sonnets for an Analyst*.

1965 *Electra* (Harcourt, Brace and World).

"The Calenders," an unpublished novella.

"Dante in 1965," *Carnegie Magazine,* May, p. 151.

Gladys' brother Bob dies.

Simon becomes manager of a housing development.

1965-66   (New Year's Eve) Her sister Dorothy dies of a heart attack.

1966   *Boris, the Lopsided Bear,* a children's book (Collier Books).

1969   "Prometheus," *Insight: Literature of Imagination,* Ed. Erwin Steinberg et al (New York: Noble and Noble).

1970-72   Gladys is Thomas S. Baker Professor of English (first holder of that chair), Carnegie-Mellon University.

1970   "Is There a Way Out for Fiction?," PLA Bulletin, January, vol. 25, no. 1, p. 5.

"Creativity in the Seventies," *English Education Today,* Ed. Lois Josephs [Fowler] and Erwin Steinberg (New York: Noble and Noble).

1972   Gladys receives the Ryan Award for Meritorious Teaching at Carnegie Mellon University.

The Godforgotten is published by Harcourt Brace Jovanovich and becomes a Book of the Month Club alternate.

Gladys dies of a heart attack (October 3).

1973   *Sonnets for an Analyst* (Harcourt Brace Jovanovich).

An exhibit of Gladys' needlework is mounted in the Old Post Office Museum, Pittsburgh.

1975   Simon dies of cancer (January).

LASTING IMPRESSIONS

Elizabeth Schmitt Culley

I like remembering Gladys as she was in the late 1930s at Sunday gatherings in the backyard of her parents' small frame house in Shadyside. At that time the neighborhood was a leafy, fairly quiet lower middle class district. A block away from Howe Street where we all lived was Walnut Street with its German bakery and Isaly's, its movie house, five and ten and hardware store. Some of the families still had old fashioned wooden ice boxes, as did the Schmitts. The coal furnaces left a fine layer of soot on the white crocheted curtains gracing parlor windows. The neighborhood had its ice man and coal truck, an Italian grocer who delivered in a horse drawn cart and a man who sharpened knives and scissors door to door. Tramps collected buckeyes from our lawns and begged sandwiches at the back door. In summertime the main preoccupation seemed to be sprinkling lawns until a sizeable stream ran in the gutters, wonderful for making dams and sailing paper boats. On Sundays there were picnics.

I could have been no more than five or six when the last of these Sunday family picnics gathered in the Schmitts' backyard, but I recall having always known that my Aunt Gladys was different from other women in the family. She was married by then, having graduated from Pitt, and had found a job with *Scholastic Magazines*. Posing her long, very thin arms and legs in the way of a dancer or a model, listening gravely to the talk and smoking almost furiously, she seemed not to rest passively, gathering strength for some tire-

Elizabeth Schmitt Culley is Gladys Schmitt's niece and adopted daughter. She is a painter and teacher who for the last five years has been working on a series of paintings of remembered interiors of her and her husband's family homes. She lives in Kent, Ohio.

23

some chore to come, as her mother and my mother did. She seemed more alert, more intense than any of us. She was clearly making more of the talk and activity than we were. My father shared her languor of pose, and with a one sided grin seemed to share her sense of irony. Her father signalled his admiration of her without having to resort to words. These mainly unspoken empathies between Gladys and her father and brother seemed to generate a subtle hostility toward her on the part of the other women. But to me, she was like the wonderful and somewhat frightening women I saw in the movies—Bette Davis or Joan Crawford—glamorous, irreverent, opinionated and verbal. Like them, Gladys seemed more brave than good, more assertive than sweet. She had an intimidating way of considering one's words so carefully as to make them grow beyond their intended importance. She could, however, break her concentration long enough to join me on hands and knees in the grass to examine an ant or invading grasshopper which had lost its way among the lawn chairs.

At that time the Schmitts and my parents and I lived in adjoining houses. Gladys and her husband Simon had an apartment across the street. We were a close family, and though Gladys was busy with her new job and with beginning *The Gates of Aulis,* no one of us was more aware than she of the currents of feeling within the family, or of the changes that each of us went through. Being a writer and having always been fascinated by people and their interactions, she had long ago assigned herself to be unofficial chronicler of the family.

The Schmitts were just recovering from the depression years, when they were terribly poor. They no longer took in boarders, but were left with a rich lore gleaned from the droll habits and odd circumstances of these lonely men. Gladys' mother and Aunt Ollie, who lived with them, had run a small candy store in their previous neighborhood, and Ollie still told hilarious stories about the children who had frequented the place, her favorite about a cross-eyed boy who never could get across to her exactly which penny candy it was that had caught his eye. Gladys' father now drove a delivery truck for the Liberty Baking Company, and her younger sister Dorothy was a secretary there. Her mother kept house with Ollie's help, but Ollie, being an amputee and more than a little eccentric, did little but make enormous batches of cookies for invisible battalions. My father, who was Gladys' brother, sold insurance.

The truly difficult times, before and during the depression, were now a memory. Gladys' parents had lived with relatives at first, moving later from one rented house to another as their family grew. Gladys' mother had taken her mother and sister into the household in order to have help with the children, but the resulting conflicts among the women proved to be more harmful than helpful in the long run. The children were frequently ill. Gladys was born an Rh factor child and was so small and fragile an infant that she was not at first expected to live. All the children had devastating bouts of diphtheria and influenza, and all had for this reason acquired the propensity for heart disease before they had reached their twenties. Gladys' father was chronically exhausted from overwork.

The tired parents, no match for their young children, unwittingly relinquished their parental prerogative in favor of the grandmother and aunt. Conflicts of authority arose among the adults, and the children were left in the midst of this ambiguous situation to make of it what they could with children's understanding. While she lived, the grandmother became more and more dominant, Gladys' parents more quiet and passive. Gladys, being the eldest child and at once the least tractable and more receptive of the children, received more than her just share of the attentions of this formidably pious, fiercely Lutheran grandmother.

Gladys had a kind of essential miserableness about her that stayed with her long after her grandmother died and the family became somewhat better off financially. Photographs of the three children with their father, taken when Gladys was about ten, show a tragic, thin-fleshed Gladys with small, dark eyes and ascetic face leaning on her father with a kind of heartbreaking adoration. She was impossible on the subject of food and would subsist on one kind of food for weeks. She even spent one entire day blindfolded just to see what being blind was like.

She was an imaginative child. She wrote poetry and painted little watercolors. She wrote plays that she and her brother and sister performed on long rainy days at home. In fact the three of them, as adults, still had a theatrical quality about their gestures and speech, no doubt developed in their childhood when they made some sense of things through drama in order to escape the family tensions which plagued them.

In high school, she felt the pressures of class keenly. She and her sister were always among the least best dressed. They despised their shabby dresses and lyle stockings and suffered from the taunts of their classmates. They were called "Toothpick and Too Thick" because Dorothy was enormously heavy and Gladys was a string bean. Their brother, on the other hand, was amiable, handsome, blithe—a banjo playing jokester, a charmer. The two girls were inordinately fond of him.

As the three approached college age, the Schmitt household relaxed more and more. Only Gladys had prepared for a career; she went on after high school to the University of Pittsburgh. The others never did go to college, partly because there still was not enough money, partly out of lack of motivation. While Gladys was in college, the house on Howe Street became a meeting place for her intellectual friends and for my father's friends too. The constant comings and goings made it the place they were all to remember as the site of good times, where there was always money for food and flowers if nothing else, and where Gladys' parents looked on hospitably and patiently, using an instinctive basic charm that could win over anyone they met.

By the late 1930s, then, the Schmitts had seen their children through the most difficult years and were ready to sit back and enjoy the arrival of the next generation, hopefully somewhere in the environs of Pittsburgh and the small frame house where they had at last found good times. But the family unity was not to last. It ended in 1939 when Gladys accepted a job with *Scholastic Magazines* in New York, and it ended even more decisively with the beginning of the war.

Gladys and Simon left Pittsburgh hoping that Si too could find work in New York, that hope becoming more urgent later with the desire to avoid the draft. Not long after, my father shocked the family by enlisting; he was sent to Europe within a year. Though her sympathies lay very much with the war and against fascism, Gladys was devastated. My mother and I moved to New York City, the first of several moves we were to make in the next years. While we were there, Gladys wrote me letters in which she tucked between the typewritten words small hieroglyphs drawn in colored pencil. For a birthday she sent me a French doll whose mauve gown clashed artistically with her auburn curls, and one magic afternoon she and Si took my mother and me to lunch at Rumplemier's tea room. But when my mother and I began to travel from one city to the next, and when my parents were divorced, by long distance as it were, it seemed a long time before we saw or heard from Gladys again.

It was during this time that Gladys completed *The Gates of Aulis*, and it is to this book I turn in searching for the young Gladys I remember, and for the family and the tenor of their lives before the war. *Aulis* is a preamble to much of Gladys' later life and work. Her interests in the pictorial arts and teaching and politics are there. Her attitudes toward men, toward sexual love and worldly success are there; so are the brooding tenderness she felt for her family and her dissatisfaction with herself, the guilt that drove her both to excellence and to exhaustion, a guilt whose roots lay deep in the past but spread inexorably into her future.

Pittsburgh, the arena of action for *Aulis,* was to be home for most of Gladys' own life. She returned there shortly before this first novel was published, to teach at Carnegie Tech. The entire family pooled its resources to buy a large house on Beatty Street in East Liberty. Gladys and Si set up a small apartment on the second floor with a music room for Si's composing and a study for writing. While I boarded at a Catholic girl's school in Pittsburgh, I spent weekends there with the Schmitts. The house had the same warmth, the same good smell of roast pork and sauerkraut as in the old days. Simon listened to the Metropolitan Opera broadcasts on Saturday afternoons or puttered at the piano upstairs. The ever-present Schmitt cat, this time an orange tabby, habitually napped inside a large glass bowl with an alarmingly small opening. As the cat grew, so did our concern for its ultimate fate. It finally curled itself in the bowl, slept, woke and panicked, and had to be extricated much as one pries the first pickle from a tightly packed jar.

Aulis was a success; it received the Dial Press Award for new fiction. Now Gladys found it easier to sell short stories to the major women's magazines, which at the time were buying stories of good quality. Simon had found work in Pittsburgh and had at last been rejected by the draft because of poor eyesight. Gladys' father and sister continued to work, and thus the cooperative household prospered.

Gladys and Simon renewed old college friends and found new ones through the university and among professional people who supported the arts. An increasing number of students visited the house, drawn by Gladys' magnetism in the classroom. She and Simon, having no children, enjoyed their company and were glad to play semi-parental roles to them. Gladys' affections were easily stirred; she formed intimate friendships quickly. But success had its price and Gladys could seldom refuse favors to her students and friends. In addition to beginning *David the King,* she found herself obligated in new ways to speech dates and social engagements, the reading of student manuscripts and a demanding correspondence. Though flattered and stimulated by these attentions, Gladys had difficulty keeping her commitments in proportion to her energies. Simon frequently interjected a word of caution. He thought it maddening that she accepted onerous responsibilities out of a simple inability to say no.

David was chosen as a Literary Guild selection; and with her check from the Guild and in expectation of mass sales of the book, Gladys bought a much larger house in Squirrel Hill, where she and her family could live more graciously. It stood as compensation for the poverty of her youth and for the hard work her parents had endured.

I came here in 1945, shortly after the family moved in. I was ten. The size of the house staggered me. It was an enchanting place with front halls and back halls and stairs both front and back, a marble foyer in the entrance, and a cavernous basement. The upstairs rooms had gas fireplaces and gigantic walk-in closets. It took days getting my bearings in the place. Gladys, too, must have explored it at first with childish pleasure.

It had been agreed by the family in general that my mother had bravely seen me along this far, and the Schmitts would now see me through high school and college. My father, having remarried and begun another family altogether, was much estranged from Gladys. They had been close in childhood, but when he visited now there was constraint, whether because of his reluctance to speak of the war or because of the circumstances of his divorce, I am in doubt. He had, however, no objection to my living with the Schmitts, and so I too was absorbed into the already complex household. I was interested in painting and it was hoped that Gladys and Si could encourage me in this direction.

Nobody foresaw that I would come to admire Gladys so intensely that after a few months in the house I would take her on as surrogate mother, nor that she would gamely take me on in addition to her other responsibilities. Knowing that past circumstances had made me somewhat precocious, she never attemped a bland or saccharine sort of mother-daughter relationship. She treated me as a much older daughter than I was, or as a younger sister to her, and took for granted that I was more discerning than most adults would have assumed. Grateful for her acknowledgment of my complexities, I gladly set aside the more childish aspects of my own personality to be worthy of her friendship. It may have been to my advantage to have maintained a childish distance from this involvement, but since there were no other children in the house and since Gladys was the dominant figure there, it was natural for me to become devoted to her.

Gladys was, besides, the most playful and imaginative person in the house. She found time to play jacks and scrabble with me and took me shopping for clothes—that most undelightful task, especially with a teenager in tow. She and Simon took me to plays and parties and restaurants, and teased my giggling friends. We had two cats, Smoky, a sentimental tom, and Milky, his fragile albino sister. Gladys and I liked to sit at breakfast and watch them playing in the pear tree outside the kitchen window.

From early morning, my life now settled into the rhythm of life in the house, which was attuned mainly to Gladys. On her days off, she woke at about eleven. The phone started ringing shortly thereafter and continued intermittently for the rest of the day. Once a week, at breakfast, the week's menus were planned, as well as the special company dinners which were becoming more frequent. Tempers tended to flare, Gladys hoping to delight her guests, her mother hoping to avoid frightening experimentation in the kitchen, the maid and ironing woman and handyman arriving usually in the midst of this, all of them lingering for a few words with Gladys who could be such fun. She liked starting the day in this warm domestic confusion, but by mid-afternoon when she had been writing for hours in the not very private living room, the pitch of activity in the house had risen to such an irritating level that Gladys could hardly find patience for the next interruption. How she endured this set-up through the completion of several novels, in addition to grading papers and making up lesson plans, I don't know. I do think it could have squelched the creative drive of another artist or precipitated a hasty retreat of some sort, but anger and frustration were the result in this instance.

Gladys was testy and indignant a great deal of the time, as much with herself as with the people who seemed crowding in on her when she was artistically at her peak. A cooler, more cautious woman might have ordered her life more to her own convenience, but Gladys, though in need of rest and privacy, could not find justification for any defense hinting at the rejection of a friend or relative. Simon aptly composed our family motto—"Bitch and Give In."

David had indeed been a bestseller and would be for months. Furniture and carpeting appeared in formerly neglected corners of the house. Gladys was swamped with speech dates and requests from charity organizations for guest appearances and autograph parties. Though it was fun, it must have been maddening too, with *Alexandra* in the works. The new clothes she packed for trips to New York were a delight to her, and the friendships she made there established her position in literary circles, but the pace was taking its toll. Her pent-up fury directed itself toward Simon, who was ill-equipped to face the barrage, not having brought this confusion upon them. He understood that she used him thus because she was most secure in his love, but he found it cumulatively injurious to his ego, nevertheless. His resentment took the form of irritation with the mannerisms in her writing. One long tragi-comic argument over her use of self invented hyphenated words lasted for weeks.

Their substantial charm and wit and uncanny ability for relaxing the natural defenses of those they met had brought them many intimate friends. But, in addition to the other pressures, Gladys and Si now faced the task of sorting out exploitative friendships from profound ones. The experience was new to Gladys. To seek out the alliance and affection of friends had been very different from being sought, as she now was. She did expect loyalty and searing intimacy from her friends, but was on the other hand gullible and trusting in dealing with strangers of questionable motive. Her heart was broken and her sense of rightness offended by people who took her affection and favors only to give falseness in return. It must be said, though, that she allowed it to happen time and again. Furthermore, her careful consideration of the compulsions and frailties of those who hurt her surely contributed to her anguish. She and Si would spend hours unravelling the motivations of some extravagant deceit when another couple might simply have decided—"Keep clear of that one, he's trouble."

Yet as the pace of life in the house accelerated, Gladys blossomed into the elegant and witty woman many of us remember, beautifully dressed, well loved, hostess of what might have been called a "salon" in another era. Brilliant new people frequented the house— artists, poets, musicians and actors, as well as research biochemists, mathematicians, attorneys, physicians. Her social and professional life revolved mostly about the Drama Department at Tech where she taught freshman English. We went to the drama productions at Tech and followed the careers of former students with interest.

Groups of students spent evenings with us, and at Christmas they carolled and came in for mulled wine. Christmas had been a special time for the Schmitts from the earliest years I can remember. It had been celebrated rather Germanically, with a tree so laden that it had to be wired to an overhead ceiling fixture, with broad red satin ribbon newly ironed each year, holding wreaths at the front door, with dozens of pfeffernusse and anise cookies stored in tins, and with the singing of "O Tannenbaum" on Christmas morning. But now we cleared the presents away before lunch and went to the kitchen to make sandwiches for the giant open house that would begin in the early afternoon and go on past midnight.

Gladys was surprisingly quiet on all such occasions. I remember her mostly sitting in her favorite chair, listening to a student or friend. Simon contributed more to the general conversation, keeping the exchanges at an intellectual level and intensity that could never approach what might be called desultory talk. Gladys felt that Si's skill in repartee and dialogue exceeded hers, though at times she was ill at ease when the talk turned vehement or downright hostile. Perhaps she wished at such moments that her influence and control in conversation had been greater. But all in all, she was proud of her home and her parties. The entertaining had not acquired stiffness or formality with Gladys' success, but retained the casual tone initiated by her parents years ago. There were always fresh flowers and good music and mountains of food, a general feeling of plenty, but never the fussy constraint that can invade the homes of the newly rich.

While Gladys did extensive research for *Confessors of the Name,* her social life continued to be demanding. Quiet evenings of talk and music seemed to relax her, and entertaining small groups of students seemed to help her gather strength; but often she would return from an evening out feeling exhausted and inadequate to the demands that had been made on her. For all her charm and elegance, she had not developed inner assurance that she could support the impression she made. Her greatest pleasure was in her work, where she had begun to feel a reassuring sense of mastery.

I wonder how Gladys might have fared had she had more freedom from the forces controlling her—if she had driven a car or gone to lunch with a friend more often, if she had vacationed alone occasionally or had some undemanding hobby. She did not have to cook or drive or shop or do any of the routine jobs that so burden some women that they have time for little else. At the same time, she hadn't the release afforded by such routine acts. Almost everything she put her hand to required extraordinary concentration and originality. She began to embroider for relaxation, first simply by sewing a crocheted chain into shapes of her own design. In no time, she had requests for tablecloths and pillow covers for friends and found her production falling behind demand.

The Gladys I remember most vividly was the striding, ironical, harassed Gladys of busy days in the fifties. She had little time to herself except to write. She seemed to be carried along by multiple duties, and by a kind of fascination with her own virtuosity in carrying them out and with the way we all became involved with her. She found time to supervise my reading. For me to get through those years without *Vanity Fair* and *Kristin Lavernsdatter*, *Madame Bovary* and *The Mill on the Floss,* Proust, Mann, and Dickens was unthinkable to her. If I came into the room when she was making notes for *Confessors,* she would entertain me with some odd anecdote or fact she'd unearthed that day. Literature and history were her passions and, being a natural teacher, she shared as much of her brimming enthusiasm with us as she could. The rhythms of her speech were in themselves lessons in poetry. The chapters of *Confessors* we read as they were completed, feeling almost as if the characters were with us in the house, as indeed some of them, or parts of them, were represented among us or her friends. When the final galleys arrived and were spread out on the dining table for correction (we had to eat our meals in the kitchen), there were days of general uproar over drastic cutting and niggling rewrite. Around that same time Gladys had word that a major film company had taken out an option on the plot of *David,* which augmented our holiday mood.

Gladys was at once at her prime and at a most dangerous point in her own adjustment to it. She sat in the garden or on the porch in between the writing of chapters, smoking, waiting for ideas to return or for her intensity to subside. Once in a while she'd treat herself to a mammoth clothes shopping expedition. In the evenings she and Si would walk around the block to unwind or go to Frenchies for lobster if she couldn't unwind. On nights when she couldn't sleep, she amused herself by reciting the English kings in order of their reign. But as I recall she was never truly idle, never lapsed into the near childish state of mind that adults can at times resort to when frustration overcomes them. Tantrums, oh yes, those she had, but play and recreation she remained without. She never wasted a good day, an energetic mood on mere play when ideas were still welling up in her, ready to be written.

During these productive years, Gladys remained deeply involved in the lives of her family. Without her willing it, we had all to some extent become emotionally dependent on her. She seemed so much more vigorous and powerful than we. If some occurrence in the family made her indignant, she raised hell until somehow the problem was solved. The growing dependence of her parents, aging and less sure of themselves in new surroundings, was to be expected. Her love for her father had always been great, he being a most understanding and stoical man. Her competitive and guilt ridden relationship with her mother, who had been an unusually beautiful and engaging woman in youth, became more complex as her mother's health and beauty faded. Simon had not achieved in music as Gladys had in literature and was dissipating his energies on advising his wife professionally and protecting her socially. Dorothy was resentful of her sister and disappointed in her own life. I was going through a stormy adolescence.

There was no one to help Gladys with her difficulties. Her health suffered, and I feel that a bitterness and stiffness invaded her writing that would not have developed without the goading problems of her personal and professional life. She began to have grave doubts about her writing and the direction it should take; she was indignant at critical prejudices against the historical novel and chagrinned at not having found a place at the heart of the avant garde, but stubbornly defended solid craftsmanship and traditional forms. She and Simon wrangled on these subjects endlessly, and out of their joint insecurities and concern for each other grew the collaborative arrangement with which they were to live for many years. Gladys had frequently sought Simon's opinion about newly written chapters, and Simon always was uncompromising and honest; but now the arguments were really vigorous, the differences between them coming into focus. Gladys' overall style and attitude were lyrical, romantic, and even a little careless at times. Simon's literary tastes were conservative; and since he was a classicist, his sense of balance was offended when Gladys gave way to excessiveness. Their literary disagreements carried over into their marriage. It was a not altogether healthy arrangement. Even her art seemed not to be her own, not to provide escape. About that time, the film option on David was dropped, but soon afterward the studio released David and Bathsheba, which capitalized on the current popularity of the

FERRAND LIBRARY
COLBY-SAWYER COLLEGE
NEW LONDON, N. H. 03257

78195

subject without employing the accuracy or good taste of Gladys' interpretations.

In 1950, when Gladys was least equipped to face it, a cloud of misfortune lowered upon her and her family. Her father, after what was thought to have been a minor fall, died from a brain injury it had caused. The loss of this most stable and forgiving man shook her inestimably. She was left alone to resolve the more difficult relationship with her mother, to watch her age without the consolation of a husband. Aunt Ollie died, after a long illness at home which troubled us all. Dorothy became seriously ill. And since, during this time of personal tragedy Gladys wrote *Persistent Image* and *A Small Fire* and started *Rembrandt,* and at the end of this period Jose Quintero became interested in *Alexandra* as material for a play, Gladys was under constant professional pressure.

She became increasingly irritable and subject to unreasoning rage. She and I had serious disagreements, mostly because, since I was now an adult, our differing ages and status blurred the lines along which our original relationship had been drawn. In these years I had completed college, fallen in love and found work in my field. These years were, had to be, hopeful for me, but for Gladys they were one ending after another. When, in 1958, Gladys' mother died and I married shortly after and left home, Gladys allowed herself to mourn the whole terrible mess of those years. Shaken and exhausted, she turned her anger upon herself, her God, on life itself.

My husband and I visited regularly, even after our work carried us to another state; but for many years, until my first child was born, our friendship was somehow crippled. She seemed to have grown in pride and anger. She was brisk and businesslike.

I recall a particularly horrifying dream Gladys had at the time, portentous in fact. She dreamed that she walked down a long corridor, in pursuit of a piteously melancholy face which glowed in the surrounding darkness. It was a Christlike apparition, suffering, lost. She woke, standing upright in the darkness of her bedroom, but saw still closer now before her the tragic face she had pursued. She had been sleepwalking and awoke to see her own moonlit reflection in the bedroom mirror, merging dream with fact. Since childhood she had identified strongly with Christ, and had, herself, facial characteristics resembling the lean, tormented faces of Romanesque crucifixes and Medieval Scandinavian woodcarvings of Christ.

Gladys' breakdown happened without my knowing. She described to me much later how it came upon her, veritably a tidal wave,

34

without warning. She was working at her desk in the upstairs study when she suddenly became victim of a flood, a giant wall of water whose undertow dragged her down where she saw the broken remnants of buildings, a city. She was consumed by terror.

She looked for help, and found an analyst who was remarkable not only for his understanding of her as an artist, but also for his ability to deal with her religiosity in a tolerant and positive way. When I visited Gladys at that time she was tenant of a wasteland of loss and despair so barren that no hope, no spark of humor could enliven her. She was putting one foot in front of the other, eating out of necessity, tolerating interruptions of her grief without much patience. The *Sonnets for an Analyst* evidence his fitness for her and also mark her passage through these terrible days. The words that recur in them like a hellish litany—a taste of ashes, taint, corruption, the biblical disasters of fire and flood—echoed the words that ruled her inner life, that lay on the top of her tongue for months. In the *Sonnets* she mourns her lost family and her lost youth and rages against injustices she endured, against those who hurt her irreparably, and against herself. In them too, at last, old sorrows and resentments are husked away. Sad as they are, the *Sonnets* do evidence a growth, a change for the better in her.

Her father she mourns more than others. He appears often in the *Sonnets,* in the first as food for Oedipal yearnings, and then (8) as one she wishes to join beneath the ground, seeing hypocrisy in living on when the only honest demonstration of her grief would be to die. The last sonnet mentioning him (39), titled "A Waking Dream," is set after Gladys' own imagined death. She meets him in the next world; the poem is a farewell, a gentle leave taking after years of denial of the fact of her father's death.

There are good reasons for the importance of this man in Gladys' life. A tall, big boned man who loved gardening, he was above all a quiet, uncomplaining man who abhorred hostility and disharmony so much that just his presence was enough to neutralize a brewing storm within the family. Even in his sixties he had the steel nerve and rocklike calm of a strong young man. He was the only rock, the steadily pointing compass of a family otherwise dominated by feminine and mercurial personalities. His neutrality was completely sincere and therefore had a curative effect upon Gladys' guilts and fears, whereas his wife's pretended blandness was betrayed by a blush or a look, indicating where her loyalties lay. He was oddly uncomplicated and had the regal bearing of a Saxon or Viking warrior. He never gave cause for anyone to dislike him. It was, in fact, as Gladys often said, he and his wife maintained at most a lordly calm, at least a hurt silence in dealing with their unruly brood.

The dreadful grandmother was the one who had dealt out justice and imprecation, who had been both protector and tormentor. An early photograph shows her seated, holding an infant Gladys, her fierce black eyes and thick black hair echoing the stiff funeral black of her perpetual crepe widow's weeds, her very bearing willing the child to live. It was she who taught Gladys to pity Christ and to feel shame for the meanness and pettiness that all children exhibit at times. In one sonnet (11), Gladys demonstrates vividly how this woman begot the guilt, pity and shame that were to become essential parts of her personality as an adult—how every personal divergence from grace became an offense toward Christ, how every merely human tragedy grew to the proportions of His suffering on the cross. (No wonder, then, that to find oneself the object of Gladys' pity was as scathing as having incurred her anger. I can remember occasions when I was surprised to find that I was not suffering as much as Gladys' solicitousness and tenderness required of me.) Clearly, this Lutheran grandmother had a deep and lasting influence. When her name came into the conversation, Gladys always raised her eyebrows somberly and found not much to say. She spoke of the family's change from the Lutheran to the Unitarian Church without much enthusiasm, as if she knew the damage had already been done her, the Gothic pose already well established in her psyche. Not until long after her grandmother's death did Gladys, in this one sonnet, allow herself the howl of childish terror she had so long ago swallowed whole.

Gladys' grandmother and mother-in-law are the furies of these *Sonnets*. Both were aggressive, frightening women whose qualities Gladys took on to some extent as a defense perhaps or out of mere suggestibility and exposure to them. Gladys was not like them at all, I think. She was actually very meek. In the *Sonnets* she portrays herself as crippled, poor in spirit, plain, with few natural gifts, little bounty to give.

Simon's mother was a very difficult person, strange and strong, almost out of control. She never accepted Gladys, would insult her and then beg for reconciliation, repeating the pattern over and over. Gladys as a young wife felt unsure of her own femininity, unaccepted by her husband's family, and inexperienced in homemaking. Her mother-in-law must have aggravated these feelings of insufficiency terribly. The resentments she sowed tainted Gladys' marriage for years. She appears in the *Sonnets* (33, 34) as a representative of hell, a tweaking, malign creature, mocking Gladys' best efforts, making them less than nothing, laughable.

Gladys' mother was, on the other hand, a soft enigma. She appears in the *Sonnets* once (22) as the sweet smelling creature who gave her a wooden peasant doll, the beautiful, fragrant mother she remembered from childhood, and once (53) as a ghost, quietly turning the latch, putting out the light, mechanically repeating the little chores that had become the very heart of her life after her husband's death. This woman was prim and old-fashioned in some ways, free thinking in others. Tight lipped and secretive about herself, charitable and sentimental towards others, she took pride in maintaining her equanimity and dignity through all storms, yet actually blushed and blanched with every changing wind. Hospitable in the extreme, she opened her house and larder to friends and strangers alike without reserve, yet gave little of her private self to her family. She cared for her eccentric sister, cooked for seven every day, and saved the best meat on her plate for the cat. Like her husband, she despised discord within the family or any kind of fuss. Suffering in hurt silence, she played the martyr again and again, goading Gladys into fits of guilt.

Aunt Ollie appears in one wonderful sonnet (40) as "the old All Fool's Day Queen," the flowering of genes gone awry, a tragic person, disturbing for her "clay-bound touch" but possessed of a fantastic personal humor made up of children's dirty jokes and misquotes of the Bible. She often played the part of nursey or baby-sitter, even to me when I was small. Childish herself, she took sides in petty arguments. She tended to defend the children, particularly Gladys, to whom she was fiercely loyal, against the adult authority of the household. She was never violent or cruel or irrational, having her own unalterable code of honor and her own hilarious version of Christian morality, but she did go to extremes. Wherever they lived, her room was a shambles of potted plants and cloth scraps, cartons spilling rag dolls she had made, drawers half open filled with broken brooches and rings, recipes tucked beneath the sofa pillows, mason jars of cold coffee and lentil soup—a kindergarten gone mad. She was prone to fits of melancholy that broke my heart. She would sit on her kitchen chair, fitted with castors so that she could push herself about with her one leg, and weep loudly, inconsolably, the childish tears pouring down her old cheeks.

Having her about gave us an unblinking tolerance for the bizarre in general, the maimed, the slightly insane. Gladys kept Ollie at home long after it had become almost impossible to care for her, and felt guilty still for having hospitalized her in the end.

Gladys berates herself in one sonnet (10) as bad wife, bad daughter, bad mother, but as even Ollie's end shows she tried hard, too hard perhaps, like a fly buzzing in the face of the immortal, as she said. It was her refusal to allow herself some excuse, some peace or respite that was so destructive to her. When she first began to see her analyst, she was surprised to discover that she had no day dreams, never had. I remember that I was puzzled by this, thinking that with her command of story line and image she would have had an active fantasy world, or that she would have at least identified with her fictional characters and their movements. Gladys, however, regarded wishes and fantasies with contempt, preferring reality at its shabbiest to any comforting dream. So, in the absence of any escape, either through self-forgiveness or pleasant dream, she became victim of the ultimate nightmare, symbolized in the *Sonnets* as fire and flood, the drowned city, the burned out brain. She and the ruined city are one and the same, the godless city and herself cleansed by the deity through final inundation.

Toward the end of the *Sonnets* (50, 51) she signals the end of her mourning. The voices of the dead fade, the endless ache subsides and a limp blessedness is left in their place. Faith, of a kind, is renewed. Being "God's dray-horse," she continues to labor in His behalf though blinded and unsure of His existence, the fact of God's existence not mattering much any more.

More than mere therapeutic release of her anger and dread, the *Sonnets* remain among Gladys' best writing. She was proud of the *Sonnets,* of the craft in them and her mastery of the form, and of the wedding in them of honestly expressed emotion with uncompromising artistic integrity. She came away from the writing of them cleansed of what she had called leprous sores, finished with the past.

A very different woman emerged from these years of grief. Though, when I visited her now with my young son, I could see that it was with sorrow that she foresaw what life held for any of us, she had begun to turn her own life around in constructive ways. For the first time she was acting in her own behalf, no longer allowing ridiculous inconveniences and interruptions. She felt deserving of the pleasures and luxuries she did have. She had learned to work out her tensions by doing little household chores, and seemed to find pleasure in them. She stitched in every spare moment and bought large quantities of good yarns. She was gentler, too. Though she had never held back before in her expressions of grief or disgust when we talked, she now seemed to want to protect me from further disenchantment with life, to keep the talk light and noncommital. With her sister and brother she made an enduring truce, though they both were to die soon after.

Outwardly, Gladys' life changed little. She kept the house and taught and wrote. She and Simon still had the kind of vitality and appeal that made young people seek them out, but Gladys herself had acquired a somewhat monastic mein, a detachment uncharacteristic of her. To see her calm and without guilt was a relief, but it alarmed me to notice that she was also very ill. As a defense, she was simply ignoring things that would formerly have infuriated her. She seemed severe and distant at times, though I suspected that the severity simply evidenced her sad acceptance of gravely altered physical capacities, precluding the ecstasies and furies in which she had formerly indulged. I do not think that she looked into the past as often, nor fed on guilts and regrets as spurs to work. She seemed to have finished with herself and with striving of any kind except to finish *The Godforgotten* and to keep her personal life unpetty and uncluttered. She had, I felt, an appalling dignity.

Seeing with what determination and resignation Gladys wrote *The Godforgotten,* it matters little to me how it stands up as literature, a novel to be analyzed in terms of plot, style and character delineation. Its statement is knowledge earned from experience, known too late; it is advice tendered as a kind of passion play for the young of our own lost and godless time. For years she had been interested in communities that had for various reasons evolved their own versions of Christianity apart from the main stream of Church dogma. The Merovingians were one such group that she had studied. Later, about the time she finished *Rembrandt* and while reading medieval history, she came across an account, no more than a few paragraphs long, of a peninsula which had become isolated from civilization through the drastic effects of tidal wave and earthquake. This tantalizing short account fascinated her and she looked for further traces of these people's history in other books. At the same time, having come full circle through days of faith and innocence to their loss, and back again to a kind of truce with God, she had concluded that such pacing and regulation as the Church provided in medieval times was psychologically healthy for most people—

that the ringing of matins, the ritual celebration of births, marriages and deaths, the observing of changes in the seasons with Christ as their embodiment, and such public and communal rites were necessary for those of us born with a sense of the cosmic joke, the nonsense of existence. Thus in *The Godforgotten* she advises, "Act sanely, order your lives, regulate yourselves and clear your consciences, but for God's sake, get on with it."

Gladys had grayed considerably and lost weight while writing *The Godforgotten*. Her swinging step had become ginger and tentative. She wore neutral colored clothing most of the time and little jewelry except for some which had personal significance for her. She was not the Gladys I had known. But to survey these last days in terms of *The Godforgotten* without considering the grace and humor of the stitchery she made at the same time would be an oversight. Being a creature of words, still Gladys transferred to yarn and cloth something for which she could find no words, a sense of line and color and symbol reminiscent of the young Gladys I remember, a sense of aesthetic play.

Upon her death, those of us who knew Gladys felt most poignantly the loss of the person, of her charm and sophistication—not to be her guest again, not to see her roam that handsome house, not to be charmed again by those elegant mannerisms, those dry ironies. But Gladys preferred always to discount herself as a woman of such and such an appearance who had won certain honors and acquired certain material possessions. Though unique and set apart in many ways from the general stream of humanity, she longed to merge with it. In the *Sonnets* (45) she wrote that her own brain, though housing a high retinue of learning, image and wit, was no more a miracle than any other human brain. Here she acknowledges her own mortality and gives the complexity of her being back into the care of the force that fostered it, sentient or senseless it matters not. Here, in this same sonnet, she reaffirms a premise that had ruled much of her life, that only human love and sharing can make some sense and worth of the enigma of human life.

A FRIEND IN NEED

Sarah Strauss

Fame had come to Gladys, in a way, even before I met her. She was the girl who made up plays in verse that were acted out at assemblies at Osceola Elementary School. We knew, too, that it was her family who made the crepe paper costumes the actors and actresses wore. Everybody in the school recognized that Gladys was someone creative and special.

We were eleven or twelve, and in the seventh grade, when we met. There was a children's concert at Syria Mosque; a teacher asked me if I would like to go with Gladys, who couldn't get from Osceola Street to Syria Mosque alone. I went to her house and we took the street car. On the way, I didn't know what to say to her: here I was, with this, to me, special person.

Gladys never felt special. She was terribly self-conscious. Because she was born with a broken ankle that healed very slowly, she had an unusual gait. She thought she was not pretty, not feminine. She had been a delicate, sickly child, so that from the beginning her parents had pampered and overprotected her. They had kept her back from school until she was eight years old, and it was not until seventh grade, by skipping several grades, that she caught up with her own age group. She was helpless in practical things like finding her way to Syria Mosque or the library in Oakland. Threatened and insecure, she needed protection in many little ways from the outside world.

We quickly became inseparable friends—I, the practical, sensible one; Gladys, the sensitive, eager one. We were the two brightest children in the class and we shared our talents and skills: I could do the arithmetic, while Gladys was best in the creative areas. And we

Except for a very short career as a music teacher in the public school system, Sarah Strauss has always been a home maker. She lives alone now and continues to enjoy music, theatre and reading.

were both shy outlanders in a way that drew us together—I the Jewess, she already the individualist.

We were drawn to each other's homes as we were drawn to each other's beings. Gladys often came to my house for dinner on Friday nights, fascinated with the warm Sabbath tradition, imagining in it a link with the past of a people. A bond grew between Gladys and my mother, who felt deep concern for her. It was my mother who saw that Gladys felt too much—too much delight, and on the other hand too much suffering. She would say to Gladys, prophetically, "You'll have an awful time when you grow up; one can't take things so keenly."

But Gladys' home and family, far more than mine, became the center of our activities, a focal point to which many of us gravitated as if it were some warm and friendly star. It began in those grade school years, when we would meet at the Schmitt house across the street from the school, early in the morning, to exchange answers to math problems. Gladys' family was there morning and afternoon to wave and talk to the children. Her parents, in fact, seemed to have no social life of their own; their home was child oriented, and they completely entered the social life of their children.

The Schmitts were a close knit family who lived in communal style, doing what they could to make ends meet. Gladys' mother, who was seventeen when she was married, never lived alone with her husband. They changed houses more often than most families, from big to small house or small to big, following their economic fortunes. Mrs. Schmitt tried to supplement the family income, but her impractical generosity and poor management played havoc with profits. When she had a confectionery-lunch counter, she made the sundaes too high; and when she kept boarders, which she usually did, she fed them too much.

Not only their generosity, but also their creative talents drew people to the Schmitts. Gladys' father, a quiet, warm man, was a miraculous gardener: wherever they moved, he transformed the back yard within a year to a beautiful flower garden. The Rabelaisian, untutored Aunt Ollie supplied the dark humor and insight that underscored every impossible situation the family got into. Both Gladys' sister Dorothy and her brother Bob were extremely bright. Dorothy, like Gladys, was a good writer. Bob's talents were social: he was affectionate, handsome, a good dancer—the personification of what was to be admired in the conventional young man.

But there were problems. Not that what went out to the world was not genuine, but that inside, something was missing. In Bob and Dorothy, it was drive. Bob was no scholar; once, in fact, his teacher called Gladys in because he was "not working up to his capacity." Dorothy never had a chance. Although she was pretty like her mother, she was obese and sickly. And she simply could not cope with being the younger sister of a precocious girl like Gladys. She retreated, I think, by leaving high school to go to an all-girl secretarial school. Gladys, on the other hand, had all the drive in the world; but she needed love, so that she was possessive and demanding of her friends and was often hard on people. Their parents were largely unavailable in these emotional matters. Their father worked long and unusual hours on his bakery route, starting at 2:00 a.m. and coming home in the late morning. By the time the children returned from school, he was asleep on the sofa. He got up for dinner, then went back to the sofa, and at mid-evening went to bed. Their mother, if indeed she sensed the deep problems of her daughters, would not face them, was incapable of doing anything about them. She had a strange kind of detached involvement with her children's lives.

It is not surprising, perhaps, that these easy-going, unassertive parents were increasingly at a loss in handling a strong-minded girl like Gladys. An early sign of her determination to have things her way came when we were still in grade school. Eugene Debs was running for president at the time, one of the many times he did so on the Socialist ticket. I invited Gladys to come with me and my father, who was a Socialist, to hear him speak at Carnegie Music Hall. The invitation created a crisis. Though her parents were active Democrats, they disapproved of Debs and would not allow Gladys to go. She raised such a furor that it was the first, and I believe the last time they took a stand. Step by step, after that, the house became the kind of place Gladys wanted to live in, where she was free to do what she wanted.

Throughout grade school and high school, Gladys and I had serious discussions about politics and religion; and in both areas Gladys' determined independence of thought came out. Our social awareness was stirred right under her mother's eyes by one of the regular patrons of the confectionery-lunch counter. We dubbed him "the wise man." He was a radical who claimed to have known Trotsky and many other prominent radicals of the time. He would come in for soup and a sandwich early in the evening. Since the atmosphere there was friendly and informal, before long we were both sitting at his table listening to stories about the economic ills and inequalities around us. I suspect he might have been a union organizer, for he went as mysteriously as he came, leaving an indelible stamp on us.

Unlike her grandmother, who gave Gladys her mysticism and strong religious conviction, Gladys' parents were conventionally but not deeply religious Lutherans; and Aunt Ollie poked fun at all of it. We talked about religion, often on long walks together, and I with my agnostic background must have been partly responsible for sowing the seeds of doubt in her mind. She was no more than twelve or thirteen when she "lost" her God. And while the aesthetic and emotional pull of the Lutheran Church always remained a part of her, she rationally became, at most, an agnostic.

In her high school years Gladys' individual interests and talents more and more clearly took on their final shape. Her love for history was nurtured by a wonderful teacher of ancient history, Miss Anna Slease. She consumed Rafael Sabatini historical novels. (Once she started, but did not finish, a novel modeled on Sabatini's work.) She enjoyed drawing and was good at it, but was discouraged by a prissy and meticulous teacher who would not give her an "A" because she "worked sloppily." Still, Gladys helped me in drawing, while I helped her in cooking and sewing; she was afraid of the sewing teacher. Gladys wrote a great deal of poetry—lyrical, romantic, purely imaginative, often about death. She had an affinity for poets who had died young; the lives of Shelley, Keats, and Chatterton fascinated her. Once, when she had been reading and dwelling on Chatterton's life and death for days, she insisted she had felt his presence in a ray of light coming into the room. It could have been no more than morbid imagination or, as it seemed then, a true transcendental experience.

She found, fortunately, substantial outlets for her romanticism and intellectualism. Even more than most girls, Gladys had romantic crushes on boys—all of them delicate and aesthetic looking—who never knew about it. But when she met Simon Goldfield, while we were sophomores in high school, she insisted he bring his friends to her house; and through him we met the nucleus of the little group that began to gather regularly at the Schmitt home, where any friend of Gladys was welcome. Food was part of every gathering; there were always egg salad and cream cheese and olive sandwiches, and home-made cookies and tea at the end of the evening. Simon's rival in the group was an artistic, poetic boy, Slavic and masculine-looking. He was in love with Gladys, and she was fascinated with him.

We were dubbed, by one of Gladys' friends, "the Schmittites." Some of us were interested in politics, some in art, and all for the greater part were interested in music. During the evening Gladys would read a few poems and then we would go on to classical records. Strangely enough, only Simon was really interested in writing, and Gladys from her earliest acquaintance with him respected his literary opinions and his criticisms of her work. We were budding intellectuals to greater or lesser degrees and took ourselves very seriously, but we were not Bohemian in any sense of the word—quite the opposite, in fact.

When we graduated from high school, Gladys received a scholarship from *Scholastic Magazines* to Pennsylvania College for Women. Because most of the girls came from upper class or wealthy homes and were not the kind of young women with whom she could feel rapport, she was very unhappy there. She endured PCW for a year, then transferred to Pitt, where she easily found friends and quickly became a favored and prominent student in the English Department. Some of the faculty took her up socially for her talent; she lived, then, in two worlds, ours and theirs. Although she had a scholarship, she also needed money for clothes and expenses, so that she marked Freshman English themes, hundreds of them, it seemed, and was able to buy herself a few nice clothes. She had always been painfully aware of her appearance, self-conscious about her clothes which were often home-made and not well fitting, and had felt hopelessly numbered among the "have-nots." Party dresses were, I think, her first purchases.

Gladys took it as a matter of course that she would have to find work after college. When she got the job with *Scholastic Magazines* and when she married Simon, she seemed to slip easily into the role of career woman. Afterwards, when I married a man who had been one of that same original group who met at the Schmitt house, we remained close, but with a difference. She seemed to have taken for granted that she would not have children, and indeed, would have had little time for children. When she worked for *Scholastic* in Pittsburgh, she used evenings and weekends for her writing, and when she returned from New York and began to teach at Carnegie Tech, the teaching and writing seemed enough. When my own first child was born and we lived in an apartment close to Gladys' and Simon's house, they came for dinner regularly on Friday evenings.

After dinner, my husband and Simon would retire to the living room for another of their sometimes vehement discussions of music, and Gladys and I would do the dishes and have heart to heart talks.

Whatever void Gladys might have felt in her life as a result of childlessness was filled by her niece, Betty. When my second child was young, we all entered upon a happy time when those Friday evenings became very special, family-like events. The three children seemed unique and charming to us all, newly entered upon parenthood as we were, without the nagging worries that accompany family life as children mature. It was an uncomplicated period, when Gladys and I seemed almost to have recreated the mood of our first years of friendship.

She was relaxed in my home, where she could walk away from and talk about the pressures of teaching at Carnegie Tech. Gladys worked very hard, and she was an extraordinary teacher. The course she designed in the 1950's for the freshman drama students— Thought and Expression, she called it—became famous at the school. She was proud of it, believed totally in the tough discipline the course demanded, and I know that she insisted that other teachers handle the course exactly as she did—I suspect she was something of a tyrant about it. In a way, her experience with Thought and Expression caused her a great deal of suffering later, in the 1960's, when she designed another freshman course for the re-organized English Department. The climate was different then; the younger teachers rebelled at the idea of being told what to teach, and the students rebelled at her disciplined approach to reading and writing. For a long time, Gladys was very bitter about this rejection, both because she had put in a huge amount of work and because any rejection, to her, was a personal rejection.

In addition, through the 1950's and 60's, in spite of what she had accomplished in fiction and in spite of her reputation as a teacher, her salary and rank at the college were shockingly low. Actually, it was Simon who complained vocally about Gladys' being exploited at Carnegie Tech. Gladys, of course, was well aware that she could have had more money and recognition in other places. But she knew, too, that she was a captive. After the New York experience, she was determined never to leave Pittsburgh again; and since she had always felt terribly hurt that the University of Pittsburgh had made her no offer when she graduated, she would never turn that way for a job. Feeling trapped, Gladys would become angry with

Simon when he complained about how she was treated at Carnegie Tech.

But no matter what indignation she felt about school, she surely found much pleasure in her relationships with her students and fellow faculty members—although these relationships, too, often led to her being taken advantage of. She surrounded herself with people, especially bright and talented young people, whose affection and approval she could be sure of. She inspired, indeed sought, the adulation of her students; for she could never overcome her basic insecurity. She insisted that everybody call her Gladys. There were many parties, and her home was open ground. So open that one deeply troubled girl moved in, while another girl came back to be married there. It was this very kind of involvement that could and did become a burden. Only in her later years, when she became so tired and sick that she had to protect herself, did she learn to say to a class, "I'm not your mother. Please don't use me as a mother."

Her tiredness in these later years, the difference in our lives, the increasing number of responsibilities we faced, the ills we suffered, left us less time for each other; but our closeness remained. I saw the family fall apart—Dorothy unwell, Gladys estranged from her brother, who had left his wife and daughter; it puzzled me—how did it happen? I saw her increasing dependence upon Simon, artistically as well as emotionally. Flawed as his humanity was, she needed his mental calibre, his courage, his reassurance. Only Simon could tell her when her writing wasn't good, only Simon could endure the pitched battles, the sardonic sarcasm with which she took his criticism, knowing that in the end she would say he was right and would take his advice. I saw her through that horrible series of losses, one on top of the other—the tragic suicides of two close friends, the deaths of Aunt Ollie and her parents, and of her sister and brother. I saw her rise to prominence in Pittsburgh and I saw the effort she made to deal with success intelligently, loyally refusing to hurt old friends, determinedly refusing to let the essential character of her life change.

It was a rich life, if not altogether a happy one. I think that, to have had success in writing and teaching, and to have married and adopted a child, and to have made countless friends in one's lifetime, is more than enough accomplishment and joy for one woman who had begun as a frail and somewhat mystical child, brought up in humble surroundings during the gray depression years.

A SENSE OF SELF: THE EARLY WRITING

Peggy Knapp

It is said that Saint Francis of Assisi, hoeing in his garden, was asked what he would do with his last day on earth. He replied that he would try to finish the next two rows. Gladys Schmitt wanted that kind of serenity and order in her life. When a loud, shrill noise woke Pittsburghers one night during the floods of 1936, most of her neighbors feared that the gas mains were about to explode, but Gladys heard the last trumpet signalling the end of the world and calling in personal accounts. It troubled her deeply that she was unready to say as definitely as Assisi had what her life task was and where her personal loyalties lay. The screeching sound in the night was eventually traced to a flooded railroad engine, but the incident left Gladys with an aftermath of neurotic fears—unwillingness to be out alone at night and worries about her health. I find this incident deeply revealing, but puzzling as well; what caused her demands on herself to be so rigorous, and what effect did this rigor have on the art she had written and would be writing during these early years?

Gladys Schmitt at twenty-seven had much to be proud of. She had been a gifted pupil at Schenley High School, a center for its writing crowd, and the author of mock-heroic poetry for its journal. At the University of Pittsburgh she had been a serious and independent student and part of a warm and lively social group. After graduation, when she worked for *Scholastic Magazines,* she was efficient and amiable, universally liked. Her outward life was decorous and by no means tragic. Many must have felt justifiable envy when she dispensed the prizes at the *Scholastic* Art Awards Jury dinner, dressed in her flattering "camille-business," an accepted personage in Pittsburgh's art community. Nor was her personal

Peggy A. Knapp is Associate Professor of English at Carnegie-Mellon University. She is the author of a book on the medieval English Bible translator John Wyclif and of articles on medieval, renaissance, and even sometimes modern writers. Her current project is a structuralist study of some early English poems and plays.

life forlorn. She lived with a deeply-loved family, enjoyed close friendships, and was being courted by several suitors.

But this busy, competent, affectionate person was not the woman Gladys saw in herself. Her world was ultimate, apocalyptic, large-gestured—the violent, but spiritual, milieu she imagined for Old Testament Israel, ancient Greece, or the Middle Ages, where commitments mattered and were tested. She wrote Don Early[1] in 1939 that dying when your life has been sharply defined and achieved is "a perfect thing. A thing that has edges. A thing that isn't messy and capable of imbibing everything and spewing it all up again, more indiscriminate afterwards than in the first place." The struggle for a hard-edged sense of herself made her impatient with the messy, shapeless, undogmatic present and receptive to the formality and stern faith of older art.

The forming of her sense of self began, of course, within the family. Gladys had been born a blue baby and was told at an early age that her maternal grandmother had saved her life by administering artificial respiration. At birth, it seemed, she incurred a debt to this powerful grandmother, and one which would not easily be paid off. Because her father, Henry, worked such long hours, Gladys remembered whole years when she saw him only when he was sleeping or at table. Her mother, Leonore, was "the most beautiful woman in East Liberty," Gladys said in "Calendars" (1965). She was not neglectful toward her children, but there was something in her friendly social grace which extended itself equally toward family, friends, and strangers, something which prevented Gladys, and probably the other children too, from feeling that they had any special claims on her love. Gladys often praised her mother's beauty and calm good manners, but in fact these very traits raised a formidable barrier to the child's acceptance of herself. She considered her own face unbeautiful and saw her own behavior as excessive and graceless. She could not take up competition for love with what seemed to her then a woman's weapons, so she substituted intelligence, talent, rigor (from the grandmother) and diligence (from her father). She always said she wrote so that people would love her.

There was the natural sibling rivalry and ambivalence in Gladys' relationship with her younger sister Dorothy, and the ambivalence didn't wear off, causing alternate closeness and resentment between the sisters throughout their lives. Her brother Bob in childhood must have received the largest share of the intense love and care Gladys always seemed ready to give, and which few others were willing, for one reason or another, to receive. There are many testaments in the stories and novels to her closeness to Bob, not all of them literally reliable. One thinks of Carl and Ellie Hasselmann in *The Gates of Aulis*, of Absalom and Tamar in *David the King*, of Orestes and Electra in *Electra*, and of course of the more nearly autobiographical short pieces "Frere," "House Divided," and "The Calendars." Most of these accounts of brother-sister love are too explicitly or implicitly sexual to give an accurate picture of Gladys' feelings for Bob, but her "desexualized" love for him remained a strong force in her life throughout her childhood.

As small children Gladys and Dorothy had been consigned to the third floor of the house the Schmitts shared with Henry's brother George and his wife. The over-solicitous mother, to avoid family conflict—she held, with unshakeable conviction, "that nobody should ever make a fuss" ("The Calendars")—kept her girls from under their Uncle George's feet. So painful was this "exile" to Gladys that she repressed all memory of it until her psychoanalysis in 1963. To face this bitter memory she composed a sonnet about it, number 16 of the *Sonnets for an Analyst:*

> There was a window—high—I could not see.
> The sun lay on the carpet—sourceless, wan—
> A certain number of hours and then was gone.
> I was in prison, and none visited me.
> Up through the stairwell music came, and calls,
> And the warm incense of the evening's spread.
> I was alone. I ate my unblessed bread
> Only with dolls and glass-eyed animals.
> It was no dream. The wallpaper, intact,
> Still shows the face that lurked in its design,
> Coming and fading, watchful and malign.
> I saw it, see it still. It is a fact;
> Otherwise, would my eyes fill senselessly
> To read: "I was in prison and ye visited me"?

The suffering of which the sonnet speaks is compounded of her exclusion from communal family life and the surveillance carried on by the glass-eyed animals and the face in the wallpaper. Somebody had judged her actions (or perhaps her thoughts) and decided she ought to be kept in prison. Somebody had discovered the wildness and excessiveness of her imagination and locked her away.

Though the "exile" itself was forgotten or repressed, the self-doubt it engendered stayed with Gladys throughout her girlhood. Several autobiographical stories and the ancestors chapter of *The*

Gates of Aulis suggest that her grandmother's response to Gladys' emotional turmoil created further unhappiness and guilt in the child. In *Aulis,* Ellie recalls a traumatic scene, surely based on Gladys' own life, in which her grandmother reproved her for thoughts and feelings which questioned God's justice. Such thoughts are natural in creative artists, but the grandmother made them seem an offense to the Lutheran God. Also, Gladys' habit of introspection and self-recrimination, the failure to incorporate that moral license that lets most of us forgive ourselves and get on with it, are surely effects of this grandmother's inflexible theology. Because of these attitudes of her mother and grandmother, Gladys at ten apparently believed herself both undernourished emotionally and at fault for her condition. When she grew up, one of her consistent metaphors for uncomplicated happiness would be a mother nursing a baby, but neither she nor any of her major fictional heroines ever bore or nursed a child.

In time Gladys' context widened to include school friends as well as family. Above all there was Sarah Strauss, her close confidante and lifelong friend. Much of Gladys' passion for ideas and for art seemed excessive and indulgent in the house dominated by the stern Lutheran grandmother, but Sarah was, apparently, willing to accept it. And I think Gladys saw Sarah's Jewishness, her link with an ancient and colorful traditon, as a more fitting accompaniment for ethical probity than the austere black-and-white outlines of her grandmother's style of religious feeling. The girls discussed their religious training and their doubts, but rational speculation was not Gladys' primary tool, then or ever, in exploring the world; imagination was. And if she could act out in mind and pose Lady Jane Grey getting her head chopped off, there was no one in her own house she could share her findings with—Sarah was alone in this nurturing for many years.

Gladys' closeness with Sarah continued into adolescence. The grandmother's strict theology (even though the grandmother herself died in 1920) was bound to complicate her transition to adulthood. Luckily by this time she had developed a way of contemplating her feelings without destroying herself—art. Her friends at Schenley High School were "a rowdy music crowd," short on social graces, but deeply responsive to music, literature, and ideas. These young people argued heatedly about whether or not Wagner was a fake, and many of them stayed together through college at Pitt to discuss whether Freud explained the world better than Marx. In such an atmosphere Gladys could both contemplate and distance her feelings. And here was the ideal audience for her early writing.

She was a poet first. Her early verse is highly polished, often done in traditional stanzas with traditional imageries. The sad shepherd, the wandering gypsy, the mortal visited in love by a fairy, the lovely maiden with a single white rose, and the phantom nature spirit figure prominently. One is reminded of Swinburn, Rosetti, or the early Yeats. The lyric gift these poems display is astonishing in so young a poet, and the range of themes, and even more strikingly of forms, is very great. But there is a huge distance from everyday life in almost all of them.

The note most often sounded, through a host of fictionalized situations, persons, and stanzaic forms, is the note of leanness, deprivation and loss. At random I can remember the opening line of "Omeric Stanzas"—"I have no love to offer you to-nite"—and of "Repast"—"Being starved for many things." The women forsaken or bereaved are many, the happily loved very few. An almost complete account of the suicide by drowning which she said she attempted in 1934 and which she writes for Ellie in *The Gates of Aulis* is prefigured in a poem called "The Unforgettable." "Late August" is typical of these poems:

> There is an autumness about this place—
>   The poplar leaves already drifting down
> And falling, thin and dry, across my face
>   And lying in the grass edged all in brown.
>
> Some maids shall dance where yellow apples peep,
>   And some shall sing where purple clusters press
> Globe upon globe, and some shall fall asleep
>   Smelling the fruity melon's mellowness—
>
> But I—(Ah, listen how the crickets rasp
>   And the sad winds creep woefully away)—
> I stand in this poor autumn place, and clasp
>   My beautiful—my beautiful decay.

Again one thinks of the romanticism of the early Yeats and of his habit, as a young poet, of presenting himself old, disillusioned, or exhausted.

But it is impossible to deny the force of the personal in the poems —it can't be international trends alone which led Gladys to contemplate despair and escape through death so repeatedly. Although firmly distanced by their formal qualities, these poems have an undeniable connection with Gladys' direct experience. "A Mystery," I was told, recounts exactly a waking vision Gladys had of the poet Chatterton. "Song" is the polished, but literal, account of a walk Gladys and Simon took through Schenley Park.

There is also a good deal of narrative poetry from this period. (Story was a natural part of Gladys' approach to poetry all along; even her brief lyrics seem expressions of a clearly-imagined character speaking from a particular situation, and many of the shorter poems were placed together in sequences, giving them a nearly fictional sense of development.) A particularly impressive poetic narrative, untitled in my copy, brings to mind Keats' "The Eve of St. Agnes." Gladys' poem is about a girl named Eulalie, daughter of a medieval baron, and her courtship by the Prince of Thessaly. Eulalie has always scorned suitors and sighed for the god Apollo, whose likeness she knows from a precious Greek vase which stands in the hallway of the manor. The story is gracefully, unselfconsciously told in the poem, no small achievment since the ten-line stanza the poet chose is so difficult technically. The effect is rightly calculated: a slightly archaic verse form used to suggest an event (much like Keats') half-way between historical romance and fantasy. The Prince who carries Eulalie away is in the end seen to be Apollo himself in disguise. This early verse-story speaks, as much romantic poetry does, of the writer's vision of another, more perfect, world, a world which makes the present seem an unsuitable place to live. In this case it also speaks, I think, of the reluctance of this perceptive young woman to commit herself to the crassness and muddle she could see all around her, when her imagination could create such Apollonian clarity.

But there is also a narrative poem, "RLM," which suggests Gladys' daily experience quite closely. Despite the rather heavy lyricism of its blank verse and the elevation of its tone, this poem manages to evoke the hominess of the table at the back of the little store her mother and aunt kept and of the nuns and children on Cedar Street. Every girl since Nausicaia met Odysseus has probably fallen in love with an older man, a stranger in her neighborhood world, but the whole rendering is new and fresh here, and Gladys celebrates its uniqueness by not consigning it to the nameless fairyland of dreams.

Many of these early poems are set in the past, often the distant past, and it must be remarked that Gladys' power to evoke and animate other eras is clear even in her earliest extant work. Her theological bent of mind gave her a deeply-felt connection with

Joan of Arc "burned up in all her majesty" and St. Ursula "martyred with her fair head high" ("to Sadila," XXIII). Such images remained important focuses for her art—whole novels are built around them and they figure many years later in her private dreams in *Sonnets for an Analyst*. The mythical and historical settings in her poetry form a disguise, I think, for the metaphysical dimension of her sense of character. The high school and college poetry presents the old problems of moral choice she had pondered with her grandmother, only now she calls the images Bacchus and Apollo and Sigismunda Maletesta. The epic, definitive gesture, irrevocable and removed from the attrition of everyday life, is transformed from the religious arena to that of myth and history.

During her college years, Gladys began to write short stories, many of them very fine. "House Divided," her first published fiction, won an award after it had appeared in *Story* magazine in 1934. The same year, the *Atlantic Monthly* printed "Saturday." Both stories bear Gladys' stamp of detailed observation, observation of the world the characters see with their eyes and observation of the way their particular personalities operate. "House Divided" focuses on the relationship between an intelligent brother and sister in a working-class household, both of them unhappy in love and unable to turn to each other for comfort. The inevitable breaking of the childhood bond between them is felt by both as a painful betrayal, and although the emotional situation is universal, Gladys gives this story in bleak, realistic, localized particulars—a cheap frame house in depression-era Pittsburgh—which adds to its powers to move us. "Saturday" concentrates on the pathetic difference between a young man's soaring dreams and his powerlessness to make even the smallest flights in waking life. Again the presentation is realistic and localized—the college department office, the marble-halled medical arts building, the shabby-genteel parlor of the elderly aunts, the streets and streetcars as the poor see them. Both stories are strongly built, using their Pittsburgh settings and their unspectacular characters to send out, unobtrusively, larger circles of meaning.

Gladys would have been happy to stay on at the University of Pittsburgh after her graduation in 1932, but the English Department did not offer the graduate assistantship she expected. Like Carl Hasselmann in *The Gates of Aulis,* she felt this betrayal was due to her capabilities rather than her deficiencies—she had already published fourteen or fifteen poems in recognized magazines. She speculated that the candor of her sonnet sequence "In a Lean Year" had lost her her place as department wonder-child. (In defense of the department, there was a depression going on.) At any rate, she gave up her graduate work to take the job with *Scholastic Magazines,* where she had had connections since she won third place in the high school poetry awards. It was a job which made use of her literary talents and also exposed her to the intermittent courtship of M. R. Robinson, a man some thirteen years her senior and the editor of *Scholastic.* Robinson's image as a man of the world (he must have made her home-town friends look provincial) and as a successful literary person exerted a lot of attraction for a young woman who had always tried to see her life under the aspect of eternity anyway. She saw in him the possibility of widening an intellectual and social scene which was getting claustrophobic. On the other hand, there was Gladys' scrupulousness about personal loyalties. Simon, Sarah, and the rowdy music crowd had a strong hold on her loyalty, having supported and understood (or misunderstood) her so long. This unresolved conflict troubled her for many years and was almost certainly a factor in her traumatic response to the train whistle in 1936.

In spite of her ambivalence about Robbie's attentions, Gladys was badly hurt when he married somebody else in 1934. The letters to Don Early give a melodramatic account of her bereaved state. "My Beloved Damnation," she calls him, and says his influence produces "something belonging to the devil—yet sweet—sweet like the arbutus which I used to carry in my purse to high school and I drew long breaths of it and thought about life-as-it-is-not-and-should-not-be" (April 1934). Thus Robbie became a character in a private romance-scenario about a loving woman who is attached to a cool, prideful lover/husband, but secretly yearns for an unattainable "other," a scenario familiar in most of Gladys' long fiction and many of her stories. I do not mean to say that if Robbie had not come into her life, wooed her a little, and then married someone else, she would have escaped imagining or writing this text. Quite the opposite: for an intense, morally alert young woman who believes herself undernourished in matters of love, it is practically inevitable that such a triangle should develop, at least in imagination. Her hopes for love were as epic as the rest of her ambitions, and no marriage was likely to fulfill them.

Robbie's "betrayal" caused Gladys to at least contemplate suicide, but she gradually brought her feelings under control, partly by pouring them into the various molds of her fiction. Until Professor

Early sent the Goldfields Gladys' letters in 1971, Simon himself did not realize how deep the wound went and how stubbornly it resisted healing. There are two short stories directly about it. In "The Mirror" (*Colliers,* 1944) the protagonist faces her bitterness over the loss of her lover to another woman and finds catharsis in her pity for a bungling waitress whose husband has been killed in the war. The story is a spare, tightly-written piece containing a good deal of sharply focused external detail. "The Mourners" (*Harper's Bazaar,* 1944) is more interior, intellectually and psychologically, telling the story of an ardent young wife who comes to see her emotion as excessive and bothersome to her cool professorial husband. For a few tortured minutes she thinks herself swept away by her melancholy piano teacher, only to reject him out of a rather morbid pity for the husband. Here the rejection is played both ways—having been turned away by the husband, the woman turns away a potential lover. "The Mourners" explores directly some very real themes of Gladys' emotional life: the passionate flare-up which might bring the woman into her fullest life, the paralyzing loyalty to the husband (Simon, suitor when Robbie married, husband when the story was written), and the cool intellectuality of the husband which rendered him unable to respond to her flights of passion or curiosity ("Now she read dismissal in the dry flat palm that patted her arm. . . . There had been many such dismissals.").

But having married Simon, she was hopeful of the quiet happiness marriage might bring. There is a sense, in her letters to Don Early, of entering a relationship whose boundaries are known beforehand; there would be few really new revelations as Gladys and Simon set up housekeeping across the street from her parents on Howe Street. They would see the same people they had before, work where they had worked, and Simon would compose music while Gladys wrote. She was not incapable of appreciating the daily joys— I think they were at least as deep a need for her as the expansive, definitive ones she was always seeking in fiction. And there are some times in these letters when she asserts her independence from both of the men in her life, ridiculing Simon for his ailing digestive tract and Robbie (still her boss in 1939) for being "God Almighty" and "a transparent fish through which the ages and all my exasperations come and go."

The move to New York to be an associate editor with *Scholastic* might have triggered another kind of adventurousness, but Gladys seemed to see the new job as a tiresome sequence of arrangements for travel and lodging. Before she and Simon left Pittsburgh, she began to coat the daily events of their family-centered life with nostalgia, and did not see herself as traveling to one of the great centers of civilization so much as she resented the pains of pulling up the only deep stakes she had. Although her work at *Scholastic* went well, Simon was restless and unhappy in his job, and both of them were glad to move back to Pittsburgh in 1941, revisiting New York only for brief business meetings. Aside from such meetings, Gladys never left her home town again. And New York seems not to have changed her as a writer in any important ways.

The faculty appointment (for eighteen hundred dollars a year) she accepted at Carnegie Tech provided a more congenial use for her abilities. She was awed by the responsibility of appearing before her classes and eager to define her role in both formal academic situations and in counseling and befriending some of her students. Many of her best stories come from the dedication she found in herself for teaching. In "The Avenger" (*Good Housekeeping,* 1945) and "Another Spring" (*Harper's Bazaar,* 1945) she reflects the Arts College at Tech directly, in the first from the student's angle of vision and in the second from the teacher's. She is good at showing the various tasks of the academic community: the husband in "The Mourners" silently preparing his lecture for the next day in the darkness of his bedroom, the penurious graduate assistant in "Saturday" facing his unfinished dissertation and his sinus pains, the drama teacher in "Another Spring" gradually coming to see her Polish student's rightness for the part of Cordelia in *King Lear.* The novels too present college teaching in strongly depicted scenes: Carl Hasselmann in *Aulis* resenting the unenlightened hierarchies of the Sociology Department; Stephen Maurer, also in *Aulis,* presenting his impassioned lecture on social change; and the entire text of *A Small Fire,* with its close accounts of department meetings and politics, classroom instruction and grading, and the sometimes warm but sometimes labored personal contacts with students. Like Chaucer's Clerk, Gladys would gladly learn and gladly teach—and she would gladly write about both.

At least three earlier experiments with long fiction were made before Gladys settled on the themes and characters of *The Gates of Aulis. Candle Saga* was a story about the tenth-century Danish invasion of England, a novel which Harper's nearly accepted for publication. The editorial board there did ask her to try a book with a modern setting, and she started one, but abandoned it before completion. Some time later she produced a short novel in the style of Virginia Woolf's *Mrs. Dalloway,* which she submitted to Scribner's First Novel contest. She and Simon heard afterwards, unofficially, that her book had taken second place to Thomas Wolfe's *Look Homeward, Angel.* She must have convinced herself in the years just after college that she could write sustained prose fiction, and with some facility.

What finally became her first published novel, though, was not facile. *The Gates of Aulis* is a long, serious, thorough fiction, begun in 1935 (a letter dated 5-15-35 says 220 pages were finished) and not out until 1942. Dial Press published it (after Lippincott had contracted for the manuscript and then merged with Morrow and rejected it; this caused Gladys another nearly-suicidal despair) and gave it the Dial Press Award "for an outstanding novel that concerns itself realistically with the problems of adjustment which face young men and women of America today." Thus the book became Important, much reviewed and much discussed.

It was an important book too for Gladys herself. A great deal of her private pain and intellectual doubt was pressed into its sturdy structure. As I see it, *Aulis* opposes two important impulses in Gladys' own personality by creating a separate character to represent each of them. Ellie is her author's striving to live responsibly and expiate guilt by caring for someone, some particular person with some particular need, in this case Eugene McVeagh, whose aging wanness needs Ellie's youth. Her brother Carl takes the social rather than the personal arena for his giving; he argues for strict self-denial, for "loving nobody, so that you can love everybody." Ellie and Carl are children of the same ancestors; they both seem deprived and they both feel guilty, though she understands this better than he does. It is true that Ellie, a woman and an artist, is more directly a self-portrait than her male, theorist brother. Then too, Carl's characterization contains some traits of others: the appearance of Gladys' real brother, Simon's unwillingness to meet emotional demands, and Don Early's coolness and intellectuality. Yet Carl's being passed over for an assistantship because of his talent and independence is very much like Gladys' assessment of why she was not asked to stay on in the Pitt English department, and Carl's angry account of Dr. Ebert is likely to be Gladys' angry retort to her one-time department chairman, Percival Hunt. If both brother and sister are aspects of Gladys, the book is about whether one serves the world better by responding intuitively to the needs of others or by developing a social doctrine which, if implemented, would benefit everybody.

Neither alternative, it turns out, works very well. Ellie's lover McVeagh, who simply needs her personal loyalty, is finally rejected when he argues an inadequate and destructive social ethic. Ellie has believed all along that happiness springs from private sources, but cannot allign herself with McVeagh's decadent paternalism and elitist pride. Carl's mesmeric teacher-colleague Stephen Maurer is rejected too, he because he lets slip his professed ideals, or never really espoused them, and confesses that he needed the support of Carl and his friends merely for his own omnivorous (and more-than-slightly sexual) ego. So both Carl's and Ellie's answers are undercut by the plot of the novel. Both pass through a time of bitter despair without being able to offer each other any real comfort.

Yet, curiously, both are saved by discarding the "father" they had depended on. When Ellie tries to drown herself, Carl instinctively rescues her, affirming in himself a simple love for a real person. This rescue frees both of them, Ellie to paint the scenes of her ordinary life and Carl to love his patient girlfriend Libby. The book does not so much solve the perennial opposition between personal service and organized social action as it does reveal ailing motives for both programs. It is the sense of guilt and voluntary self-deprivation that is finally exorcised by the conclusion of the novel. When Ellie paints her loveable old failure of an uncle Paul, she affirms the goodness of her own origins, and when Carl makes love to Libby he acts out of unashamed acceptance for his feelings and hers. The phrasing of the conclusion is a distinct case of what Lionel Trilling called "lumpy lyricism"—a later Gladys Schmitt would have found a lower key for the last speeches—but there is wisdom and vision in these affirmations in spite of their overarticulateness.

There was abundant and intelligent discussion of *The Gates of Aulis* by some of the most respected critics in the country. Even those who liked it least recognized its seriousness. The praise ranged from comparisons with Mann and Proust to acclamations of a totally new talent and even of a new kind of talent. Every reviewer noted the "heightened prose" and commended it when it worked; most noted that it didn't work all the time. Lionel Trilling claimed that in conveying meaning *Aulis* places too heavy a burden on the style and too light an emphasis on story, which he none-the-less saw as quite strong when looked at from a distance.[2] Clifton Fadiman said what amounts to the same thing when he found the verbal analysis the characters engage in too ponderous (though often brilliant in itself) for their actions.[3] In general, the critics found in *Aulis* an excess of verbal talent, an excess of passion and moment. Excessiveness had always been Gladys' problem. Like the glass-eyed animals and the face in the third-floor wallpaper, these critics accused her of too much—too many words, too much insistence, too much predicated on the unimpressive Pittsburgh actions she had chronicled.

What is missing in the reviews of the 1940's is an appreciation of the strength of the novel's conception. It is true, I think, that there is something claustrophobic about *The Gates of Aulis*—Robert Littell (Yale Review)[4] wished that such an intelligent writer would "open the window" on her stifling vision of the present. But it is equally true that the young people in the imagined world of this fiction were betrayed by their elders and do feel trapped—that's the whole point. We don't attribute to Joyce Stephen Dedalus' morbidity, his romantic excesses, or his intellectual arrogance, we praise the author for creating these states authentically. Gladys' fault in *Aulis* is not that she writes about trapped characters, but that she does not make the larger arena of her own perceptions and sympathies clear enough, does not convey strongly enough the compassionate irony with which she sees this brother and sister. This is a technical difficulty, since she chooses to let only Carl and Ellie convey point of view, and they are too much alike to "open the window" on each other's maladies. And the charged, lyrical prose is better suited to the truly demonic Stephen Maurer and the ancestors in chapter three than to the more limited scope of life in Pittsburgh. Yet although they are dramatized in immature, self-regarding characters, the big moral issues of the period do inhere in *Gates of Aulis*, and the structure of the novel really illuminates them. Dial Press was not wrong to see in the novel both scope and realism. And Gladys' career in long serious fiction was launched.

NOTES

[1]The factual material here is derived from four sources: a series of twice-weekly interviews with Simon Goldfield after Gladys' death, conducted between September

and December 1974; some thirty letters from Gladys to her college friend Don Early (now Professor Early), dated 1933-1959; Gladys' own unpublished poems and stories; and her published work, including the novels, the sonnet sequence, and the many short stories which appeared in magazines during the 1940's and 50's.

²"The Use of Ideals," *The Nation* (May, 1942), p. 547.

³"Enter Gladys Schmitt—High Strategy," *New Yorker* (May, 1942), pp. 56-57.

⁴Review of *The Gates of Aulis, Yale Review* (summer, 1942), p. viii.

THE MARRIAGE

Lois J. Fowler

Gladys Schmitt's marriage to Simon Goldfield in 1937 marked the beginning of a commitment that endured to her death thirty-five years later. To those who knew them well in their later years their life together seemed often gay, sometimes tortured, always loyal. I knew her as fellow teacher and friend, and Simon likewise as friend. The portrait of a marriage which follows depends largely on my perceptions of them in those later years, partly upon the reminiscences I heard from them and from others. These impressions convince me that for Gladys, from first to last, life with Simon fed her intellect but left her emotions hungry. She found herself tied to him, and he to her, in profound dependencies that produced as much frustration as gratification. The woman and writer can each be only dimly understood without these considerations in mind.

Since earlier chapters have revealed much of the personality and powers of Gladys Schmitt, let us turn first to Simon Goldfield. These are excerpts from some appreciative words spoken at his funeral, fifteen months after Gladys' death, by his friend David Fowler:

> . . . Some of Simon's talents—the sorts of things for which one hopes to be remembered—never flowered fully. His abilities as musician, expressed in performance, composition, and teaching, did not escape the restraints of his perception that he himself could never meet his own standards, which were of the highest. Yet his aesthetic appreciation in music grew to be broad, deep, and accurate, making him a worthy commentator and critic, a joy to listen to and debate with by those who knew the field.

Lois Josephs Fowler is Associate Professor of English at Carnegie-Mellon University, where she teaches courses in advanced writing, teacher training, women's studies and the Victorian novel. She is currently working on a short biographical article about Ann Trow Lohman, 19th century abortionist, and with her husband, on a biography of Jane G. Swisshelm, a 19th century abolitionist and journalist.

His abilities as a translator, expressed in his *Medea* and his unfinished *Iliad,* emerged only in his later years. In his own eyes the chief virtue of his work was to produce a more harmonious sound and a happier realization of potential, to bring clarity and grace out of obscurity and awkwardness. Behind the translator stood the musician.

This clear understanding of structure, balance, economy, appropriateness, direction, and resolution served both him and Gladys well in his role as reader, editor, and critic of her work. No one knew better than she the ways in which his perceptions and challenges contributed to her great achievements. His belief in her greatness—the obverse of the coin of his devotion to her as a person—led him to continue, after her death, to explore her novels systematically, with the help of friends, so as to encourage critical attention to her work. . . .

The rest of the eulogy recalled Simon's administrative talents, his wit and perception in conversation, and his concerns for friends and friendships. Those few of us who listened at the grave on that raw January day found irony as well as poignancy in both the occasion and the remarks. We mourned his loss while remembering the dearer figure of his wife. We savored our friend's virtues as recited in the eulogy while reflecting on the significance of the failings at which it hinted. We understood that Simon's talents "never flowered fully" through fear, the inability to take risks, to do battle. We knew that his unfinished *Iliad* remained unrealized as a translation because of his inclination to retreat from conflict rather than to resolve it. We recognized that his drive "to explore her novels systematically . . . so as to encourage critical attention to her work" expressed genuine belief, no doubt, but also a compulsive need to sustain his own ego, fragile unless it could draw strength from identification with the successes of Gladys. If he was wise, perceptive in counsel, astute in criticism, and eager in helping his friends, these qualities grew not out of heartfelt sympathy but rather out of his acute need for dependable companionship. While crediting his skill in advising us how to meet problems, we remembered the intense, caring warmth given to young friends by Gladys, who cried in the *Sonnets* (24), "And who put out my fire?" Was it Simon, who long before had turned his own fire into ashes?

Looking at these ambiguities in the man, I ask what it was that held Gladys to Simon, and how the marriage really went. There are clues in their earlier lives together, about which it is relatively easy to speak objectively, and in Gladys' literary work, where one needs to be more tentative.

When Gladys Schmitt and Simon Goldfield met as high school students, she the precocious writer, he the talented musician, they shared the zest of intellectual comradeship and the fun of speculating about their future roles in the cultural elite. Within the circle of congenial friends at the Schmitt home in Shadyside, outside realities, even those of the Great Depression, could be forgotten. That home, through their college years and a lengthy courtship, was their retreat. Later Simon would sometimes muse wonderingly at the way in which a sort of voluntary "slave labor" on the part of Gladys' mother and aunt had produced food, service, and comfort for them and their friends at any hour, with unseen hands preparing meals, washing dishes, and restoring order. There too they found a kind of sexual tolerance, symbolized by Gladys' father leaving quietly to service his bakery route in the early morning, ignoring the two figures sleeping on the sofa. Perhaps it was the safety of this insulated world that allowed Gladys and Simon to play at being young lovers for so long.

That game and the marriage which followed included a Jewish mother-in-law as one of the players. Simon's mother objected to her son's involvement with a Gentile, and though she appears often in the *Sonnets* as an object of humor, she battled insidiously for possession of her son. Simon seemed at the time to be flaunting his repudiation of background and of his mother's will, yet he may well have revealed in other ways, on a level that a sensitive Gladys unquestionably would have perceived, the tuggings of the psychic umbilical cord. Their expressed motive for delaying marriage for so long was their need of money, but Simon's difficulty in formalizing his break with mother and tradition must have counted too. It is surely significant that in their later lives, when I knew them both well, the shade of this long-dead "tigress mother" (Simon's words) haunted their discussions so often. In the *Sonnets* Gladys captured her sense of an unending battle lost—"If I could break her stranglehold, I'd only stumble on her noose and hang . . . "—with her resulting exhaustion of emotions—"I'm much too tired to elude you any more" (33). On his part Simon could express his sense of his mother's limitations—"When she read *Sons and Lovers* she couldn't see anything wrong with Mrs. Morell as a mother"—while at the same time refusing to take Lawrence seriously as a writer, even in his depiction of a character like Paul Morell. Simon spoke of what he called "the Lawrence cult" with more bitterness than the subject deserved. It may be that a Lawrencian shot had struck too close to one mother's son.

Perhaps because of this interference by his mother, as well as for other reasons, Simon never fulfilled Gladys' hopes and expectations for physical love. She blamed this failure largely on what she saw as her unattractiveness. Martyr to her unfavorable comparison of herself with her conventionally beautiful mother, to whom her father was ardently devoted, she maintained to the end of her life a disbelief that anyone could find her an attractive woman. That Simon and Gladys, in spite of this, succeeded in finding so much happiness in the earlier years of their marriage owed much, no doubt, to their strong youthful vitality and to the security of extended family life with the Schmitts.

After the few "daring" years alone in New York, without immediate family supports and with fewer friends, Gladys and Simon returned to Pittsburgh, significantly because Simon lost his job with the National Refugee Service. I was never able to pin him down as to why; Gladys said that her job with *Scholastic Magazines* interfered with her writing. I suspect, however, that living without family, even given their youth and dreams, strained their relationship. It was, in fact, easier to come home: Gladys to the faculty position at Carnegie Institute of Technology, Simon with the rationalization that it made sense for him to continue with his study and teaching of music at home, where he could also function as Gladys' editor and begin to work toward his new goal, a translation of Homer.

On the surface, life was more than bearable, optimism growing when *David the King* was selected by the Literary Guild and the flow of royalties allowed them to buy the large and gracious house on Wilkins Avenue in Pittsburgh. It was a house enlivened by activity: Gladys' parents, aunt, sister, and young niece found physical comfort in the surroundings and emotional comfort in performing their familiar roles as family and caretakers. Simon found a retreat from his abortive attempts at earning money or prestige and moved from his declining fantasies about his own success into a growing involvement with Gladys' success. Gladys found the needed freedom from household chores, the astute critic in Simon, emotional supports from family and friends. Years later, I remember Simon, rarely a sentimental man, indulging (and he would have called it so) in nostalgic sentiment about the open house at Halloween, the gathering of friends at Christmas and other holidays—a life in which aloneness was never experienced. If an undercurrent of strain showed—too many neurotic somatic symptoms, increasing hypochondria, erratic eating patterns, hypertense activity especially with Gladys—it was muted by the physical comfort of the Wilkins Avenue home. What existed in the present would seemingly always continue to exist; and though now in 1977 I find it difficult to understand their inability to prepare for inevitable losses, I also recognize that life then must have held the euphoria that tended to characterize the years after World War II. Losses, however, began to occur with the death of Gladys' father and they continued with increased rapidity so that Gladys and Simon were finally alone, faced with marriage, in a real sense, for the first time.

Thus we can see the logic of the psychological breakdowns when they came. The warnings—the symptoms—began to appear earlier. There was Simon's indefinable trouble with eyes in 1959—at times he could hardly see and feared blindness. There were Gladys' eating difficulties, now increased to manifest what appeared to be a state of physical exhaustion. In spite of these problems, *Rembrandt,* with its telling portrait of Saskia, appeared in 1961. It received favorable reviews but sold only moderately. The tremendous disappointment was perhaps the immediate traumatic cause of Simon's collapse into debilitating states of anxiety and depression that demanded constant reassurances from a psychiatrist and from a vulnerable Gladys, for whom even a less-than-adequate sex life had now become nonexistent. Surprisingly, she seemed strong through months of this, working when she could between Simon's states of rejection, manic dependency, and hysteria.

Her subsequent and sudden collapse was inevitable. As she later described to me what happened, she likened her state to that of Father Albrecht in *The Godforgotten* when he unknowingly ate the spoiled grain containing ergot and hallucinated into sickness. Gladys talked often about her break with reality: her vision of herself in the center of the room, not a room that she knew but one that whirled around as she moved with it—humming, seeing objects not there, giving herself to the complexities of her confused inner world. After this event, she entered the therapy which released the depression so long and deeply held in. Now she began to suffer more openly and immediately, with no external supports.

How did the marriage appear then to those of us who watched the anger, the anxiety, the depressions and the symbiotic tenacity that determined final acceptance of their life together? Simon did get a job as manager of a housing project where, as he so often said, he was able to develop surrogate, extended families depending on him for authority and support. His needs for recognition rested on and were largely fulfilled by Gladys' work. Gladys, taking the more difficult route, struggling with therapy, chose to explore within to discover her own strengths and weaknesses. But as the *Sonnets* so clearly reveal, she never could transcend dependency in order to break or even alter the established patterns of her life. Simon's job, far less demanding than hers, allowed him the energy to run the home: to shop, to plan for parties, to call repairmen, to negotiate with the housekeeper. Gladys settled knowingly but increasingly for his services and his devotion. Simon always woke earlier than Gladys; and when she woke, there was always orange juice freshly squeezed, coffee freshly ground and brewed, with hot rolls, for her breakfast. Certainly, he would transport her from school promptly at five, surprise her with small, inviting snacks to tease a reluctant appetite, comfort her with the appropriate house-coat and slippers and dinner following a particularly arduous speaking engagement.

Hostility about this seeming reversal of roles never came to any satisfactory resolution: Gladys was unable to accept; Simon, to relax. She managed to sublimate in her work. She treated herself to special favors: buying expensive clothes in too great quantity; enjoying the beauty parlor every Saturday, but only when it became clear that Simon approved of the hair style. On some levels she continued angry—not fulfilled in love and sex, too involved with work that did not include writing—and continued sending barbs in Simon's direction.

Both expressed concern for the future: Simon's job had only a small pension; Gladys', not too much larger. Most equity was in the house which had increased in value. If both retired—and the time was not too far off—it seemed likely that they would have to sell the house to have sufficient capital to continue their way of life.

Underlying tensions fused with brilliant, witty conversation so that even formal evenings at the Goldfields were always fun. Informally, one could usually find a genuine welcome. And it was the informal evenings that I remember as most significant. If undercurrents of antagonism surfaced in clever, sharp exchanges, still a friend's mind was challenged by ideas tossed about, one's psyche invigorated by the conversation: Simon's extemporaneous limericks, Gladys' engaging, funny stories. And they could usually listen to the problems of others; advice came easily yet sensibly and perhaps even brilliantly. The evening was predictable, always the same, yet never dull. One tended to relax, even to join the ritual with Gladys always in the same chair, her needlework on her lap, the cat beside her, comfortably, happily, lovingly trying to get under Gladys' constantly moving hands. Simon usually sat on the couch with one arm over the back—helpful to his gastritis, he would say. Rituals were always played out: tea (hot or iced depending on the season) in the large kitchen around the Nakashima table, tea that Simon brewed along with snacks of cheese or leftover spreads; Gladys' tranquilizers; the sleeping pill for both. Taking the pill marked the end of the evening for guests, the start of a short period of listening to music alone together.

Simon had long since given up the piano; it was no longer in a house which could have easily accommodated it. But he could not sleep without a period of listening to music. Gladys, an edge to her voice, often suggested that he get earphones, but he insisted that she share this part of the evening with him. She did so while working furiously at her needlework. But I suspect she also enjoyed that part of their life that was so totally private, that evolved into a sharing of hobbies. After the music, the two of them slowly walked the long curved steps to a double bed which held them (and they both described their sleeping patterns) curled up together in the one way they had learned to be really close.

With their social life under control, their emotional life fluctuated between moments of genuine affection and moments of intense anger. Some of these, even her sexual frustrations, Gladys spoke openly about when we had rare and intimate lunches together. Yet however depressed she may have been at lunch, any suggestion that she leave Simon met with silence. And Simon still functioned, strongly as ever, as critic of her writing, which was always, now as in earlier years, related to her emotional life. She was working on the *Sonnets*. Ironically, Simon never objected to the intimacies they revealed—probably because he saw them so inextricably bound to the work of art, the sonnet form, easily interpreted in a variety of ways.

Not so with *Electra* which, simultaneously with working on the *Sonnets*, she wrote in six weeks, a speed unheard of for Gladys, whose care and precision were unmatched. Deeply absorbed in myth, she planned a trilogy of her own, *Electra* to be first. Simon disliked it and the trilogy remained a dream. He saw the novel as careless, sloppy, flippant—perhaps as too openly revealing. Simon put his hand on *Electra* and Gladys was unable to disregard that hand, to combat openly her critic, who protected her in ways that she could not protect herself.

As one looks at the Goldfield marriage in comparison with the Schmitt portrayal of the relationship between Clytemnestra and her lover Aegisthus, it does not seem strange that Simon disliked *Electra*. He had his critical reasons, of course, but they were never clearly defined. And how *could* he react in a positive way to Aegisthus, an aging, tired, defeated man whose dangling testicles hang, too much used by life? How could he react to Clytemnestra, as she like Gladys suffers the disappointments of unfulfilled love? Clytemnestra has devotion, yes—but excitement, romance, no. She is caught between the exaggerated ego of Agamemnon, a man of war but never love, and Aegisthus, a man of devotion but not of love. Aegisthus and Clytemnestra, as Gladys describes them, represent death, not by fire, but the ice of disillusionment.

Gladys' need for affection demanded constant reassurance, consistent physical demonstrativeness; but she compromised for genuine devotion. She had in fact learned early, and written long before this, of the pain of renunciation. In a short story written in the mid 1940's, "Consider the Giraffe," Gladys, always a master of point of view, explores the thoughts and emotions of a small child at the zoo where she inadvertently watches copulation, then realizes suddenly that her beautiful mother and her admired father engage in similar activities. She is captivated by something she cannot fully comprehend but needs and wants. Her aroused emotional state frightens her parents, who misunderstand her fantasies. When her father shakes his head in puzzled comment about their experience at the zoo—"You certainly made an ass of yourself over that animal"—her mother replies, "But doesn't she always?" The reader sympathizes with the child, jealous, confused, in conflict, feeling so unloved—even approaching the tragic, in the final lines of the story: "Her mother coming in to see that she was well covered on the winter nights wondered why she always fell asleep with her hand pushed hard against her lips."

Versions of the same kind of relationship, the entire psychological history, are depicted in the *Sonnets*. Simon, the analyst, others, she sees initially as parasitic, as exploiting her: they do not work as she does, they take her money to listen to her words. Sharp lines express her emotional frustration: "A practiced masturbator" (Sonnet 7): or, what must be a direct shot at Simon, "Come, ghostly

69

gigolo, and bless this night with brainless aim-inhibited tenderness" (Sonnet 13). She sees herself as "Ill-paid, ill-used, ridiculously dressed" (Sonnet 17). She directs early and current angers toward her analyst: "I pay you, and it stabs me in my guts," because "Money is shit" (Sonnet 19). Has anyone ever loved her, provided her with needed attention for a reason other than her success and money?

But whatever she discovered now—her sense of ugliness, her inability to seek illicit sexual love, her incapacity to live comfortably alone, her intense need for what Simon could give—with understanding came a measure of acceptance. She knew that she must learn to live with Simon and a marriage that promised little change— no greater satisfactions—no return to youth. Thus she describes in the *Sonnets* (69) "The only grace I have, the grace to grieve/Without the drugs of self-deception." Simon, to a large extent, settled metaphorically for those drugs and so they lived.

Gladys, the sensual, gifted writer, was finally the unaggressive, traditional woman, who wanted love of her body, but Simon could not give her, or anyone, that love. Both mothers stood in the way; hers, the model of femininity, admired and coveted by her husband; his, the model of possessiveness, holding and pulling even in death. It is the confession of this fundamental need and denial that appears in the *Sonnets*. (Ironically, in the *Sonnets* we find early examples of the new confessional literature that so many women are writing today.) And though her spoken advice to us—younger women, searching also—was feminist in every sense, for her it seemed better (and possible, after her psychoanalysis) to dream of affairs that never happened, to engage in vicarious emotion by mentioning them enigmatically, and to allow Simon to care for her in devotion, not love.

I cannot help but speculate about how different it might have been had Gladys, with her drive, her talent, her personality, her needs, been the man and Simon, the woman. In that case, would the world have seen her early death as a direct result of her complaint that she was overworked? Would the world have seen Simon, not as the unsuccessful husband, but as a loving, caring protective wife? Would Gladys and Simon themselves have had such difficulty in their marriage? For whatever they understood intellectually about this reversal of roles, they could never fully accept it, so they adjusted to it by idiosyncratic forms of retreat: Gladys to portrayed fantasies of a great love affair (Julianne in *The God-forgotten*) but also to that realistic vision of final acceptance that emerges in the *Sonnets;* Simon to his identification with Gladys' success, to his hypochondria, to his rituals, to his nurturing role. What a complex, and yet somehow tenacious and productive symbiosis was this marriage.

MEANS AND EXTREMES: THE WOMAN WRITER

Pamela McCorduck

It's human destiny to be in torment, pulled without mercy between needs of the spirit and needs of the flesh; between pity for ourselves as a species and utter revulsion; between autonomy and submission, arrogance and humility, self-fulfillment and self-sacrifice. No human being escapes this earthly rack, and death is the only resolution.

Such a bleak thesis dominates both the first and last of Gladys Schmitt's published novels, *The Gates of Aulis* (Dial Press: New York, 1942) and *The Godforgotten* (Harcourt Brace Jovanovich, Inc.: New York, 1972). Though thirty years elapsed between the publication of these two books—and there were seven other novels besides—the thesis endured in Schmitt's art, and surely in her life as well.

Of course they are the persistent themes of Western ethics, from Plato to Augustine (referred to both in novels and in her posthumously published sonnets) to Harvey Cox. The assumption that these sets of opposites are irreconcilably opposed informs most of our institutions—the church, the law, the family. Germane to this examination of Schmitt's work, however, is another assumption. It's that one set of these opposites, namely, spirituality, pity, submission, humility, and self-sacrifice, belong or are especially appropriate to women. We're not speaking here of a middle way, a balance. For human, as opposed to feminine, behavior, we understand that a balance between these opposites is essential, and the weights on either side of the scale are an individual matter. To embrace life, not death, resolves the conflict for us; life lived with appropriate amounts of everything. We dream of entering into our old age with all our capacities intact, nourished by a long

Pamela McCorduck is a writer on the faculty of the University of Pittsburgh. She has written two novels, Familiar Relations *and* Working to the End, *a non-fiction book on computers called* Machines Who Think, *and many short pieces.*

history of the exercise of them all.

Appropriate feminine behavior, on the contrary, has traditionally insisted on the extremes. Women are to be as compassionate and sexless as the Virgin Mary, as long-suffering as the patient Griselda. I use old myths but the impulse is hardly dead: Patricia Nixon survived on the "Most Admired" lists long after her husband's disgrace, and very probably because of her public behavior during it. She was always loyal and silent. So the shrew will be tamed, Annie Oakley will fake incompetence, and one more thing—it had all better happen before the age of 35, for an ugly old woman is a double offense to nature, and if we no longer burn her as a witch, we roast her with thoughtless jokes or freeze her into invisibility.

The essays in this book show that Schmitt was deeply aware of this "appropriate feminine behavior" and of course deeply opposed to its human injustice. For example, Peggy Knapp describes Schmitt's anguish at not being offered a fellowship at the University of Pittsburgh when she graduated from there. "Somebody had judged her actions (or perhaps her thoughts) and decided she ought to be kept in prison. Somebody had discovered the wildness and excessiveness of her imagination and locked her away." Her candor gave offense, Schmitt felt, because candor is never silent, but King Lear would rather hear Regan's and Goneril's flattery than Cordelia's loyal truth. Schmitt was battered by this lesson again and again: the graduate fellowship is only one example.

So while she was aware of the high price she was paying every time she violated the canons of appropriate feminine behavior, and as she gradually learned to dissimulate in order to keep from offending the divine right of kings and also in order to survive, her view of the world, as expressed by her characters, seemed to say that balance is impossible.

Men and women in both her first and last books struggle with the conflict between their sensuality and spirituality, always naming the flesh as adversary to instead of part of their better selves.

In *The Gates of Aulis,* Carl is afraid of and disgusted by flesh, sure it will deflect him from the great mission he sees for himself as a labor organizer and a disciple of his professor, Stephen Maurer. When Carl's sister Ellie embarks on an affair with an older man, Carl's disgust is bitter and explicit. Schmitt almost seems to share it, for Ellie can have love and sex, but not art too: during her affair with Eugene her painting suffers. In the climactic scene of the novel, brother and sister confront each other with their disillusionment and misery. Maurer, it seems, has only wanted Carl's flesh after all, not his high ideals; and Ellie's lover has deserted her for a more gracious, more beautiful, but probably less passionately intense woman. Partly it's Ellie's doing. She confuses love and pity and can only fall in love with men when they are somehow physically flawed. Her first lover had died of tuberculosis, her grand passion in the novel is old, too old for her; he is sometimes described as querulous. It's as if her own lack of grace and beauty—an artificial standard she can mock and yet at the same time yearn for—makes her pick only men she can pity, thereby extracting some extra tolerance from them for her own lack of physical beauty. "Is there something more you want?" she cries to Eugene as she sees he will leave her. "Is it because I'm not beautiful? Love me, and I'll be beautiful. Whenever you love me, I grow a little riper, a little better. I think I could be very beautiful if I had any sureness in your love" (575).

There's a cry from the heart. It's more catastrophic for a woman in our society to believe she's unbeautiful than to be childless, or even arrogant. However much a woman like that knows that beauty is something contingent on time and place and circumstances, that it's truly in the eye of the beholder, she's made to feel flawed, undone, unfinished, not good enough. She can't help believing she'd better make an extra exertion to earn love, because she has no natural right to it.

Julianne, the chatelaine who is the main female character of Schmitt's last novel, The Godforgotten, also considers herself un-beautiful, but the reason here is age. Longing for Albrecht, the priest who has come from the mainland, "She wished she could see him with the sleeves of his cassock rolled up—she had not seen his arms bare since he had held them out to her in his delirium. Dry arms with stringy sinews, old before his time—why was it that *his* age carried for her no taint of disgust? And hers for him? Covertly, as if she had an itch of the skin, she ran her fingers over her throat. There were better throats in the village, full-fleshed and moist" (158).

The conversation at that moment is about despair, and Albrecht asks Julianne if she has ever felt it. Yes, she answers, and adds silently to herself, yes, with the line of my breasts subtly changing, with the flesh of my throat drying, with whatever I had of beauty wearing away and whatever I had of hope remembered only to make a fool of me. Julianne's hesitation to enter into the relationship comes not so much from the violation of the marriage vows—

she's lonelier in her marriage than she can bear—and not so much from the violation of Father Albrecht's vows of chastity. Rather, she imagines herself unlovable because she is unbeautiful, that is, aged.

Albrecht's views of Julianne are somewhat different. She appears first to him in his fever as the ministering angel, a pair of hands "so well formed and carefully tended that he confused them now and again with the ones he had dreamed of back in the Chapter House: almond shaped nails, long fingers, veins showing through delicate skin. This second pair touched him tentatively, the eloquence of their compassion held in by a wincing fear of hurting him or putting him to shame." Later: "She of these long, hesitant fingers—what sort of woman was she? Not since his infancy—he believed he could remember the touch of his mother—had he dealings with such giving hands" (68-69).

At long last he sees her. "She was made after the manner of the ancient wooden likenesses of God's mother that were carried in ritual processions—smooth and round of brow, with breasts delicate yet swollen as with holy milk; narrow of waist and slight of hip— it had been established by the learned scholars of the earliest days that Mary never lost her youth, but received her crucified Son in the same body that had borne Him, marked with sorrow, yes, but still in the April of her days. She moved lightly around the table, looking down at the blocks laid out by the two monks. The candlelight that shone down on the board shone up in her face. There were hollows in her cheeks and temples, and the light brown of her hair was muted, probably greyed. No, she was older than the Virgin, but the careful timidity of her bearing gave her the air of a child" (71).

A ministering angel, the virgin, an eternal adolescent. These are perhaps appropriate delusions of a raving man of God. But there's nothing to follow which corrects the vision. Instead, it's annotated, expanded. The first time he hears her voice and recognizes it as hers, she is "flirtatiously pleading" with her husband to be allowed to let something—a madwoman, it turns out—stay for a while in the garden. Julianne cajoles, Julianne wheedles; Julianne imagines but can never express anger.

If there are ministering angels there are also avenging ones: coming from a night of love with Julianne, Albrecht is met by the madwoman who had discovered their love, and who stabs him in her rage. Though Albrecht is near death again, he recovers, and this time resolves to take Julianne with him away from the island and start a new life. He sends her a note proposing this.

Her answer is no, and she gives him three reasons why. The first is compassion for her husband Alain. He is close to distraction, perhaps suicide, over her infidelity (though the careful reader wonders why—he's hardly paid attention to her for twenty years). "And desire at the expense of compassion," Julianne writes back to Albrecht, "would work a more ruinous change in me than that which I must choose: compassion at the expense of desire" (299).

The second reason is the example she must set for the unborn. "Let them say of me at a time far off: In that cell lived one called Julianne, the chatelaine, and she broke the holy law most flagrantly with one named Albrecht of Cologne. But he went from her afterward into his own country and did whatever he could to cleanse himself before the Lord, and she remained in the nunnery and in the end was absolved, after many years of penitence. And it will be a foolish tale, no more to be taken wholly into a wise heart than the virgin Genevieve's vision of the drowned Cathedral or the Abbot Benno's thornbush; yet it will be nourishing to the children, since it teaches, together with the immutability of the law, the sweetness of absolution" (299).

The third reason harks back to her original hesitancy. "We have been fortunate in that we have harvested in the ultimate hour. What could we desire that we have not been given? What could be revealed to us that we do not know? . . . . I am everlastingly as I was in Jehanne's hovel, when the dawn awakened you and you awakened me, yours for all time, Julianne" (300).

No Iphigenia ever sacrificed herself so willingly. Never mind that Alain had left her lonely and physically bereft for twenty years; never mind that proof of the mutability of the law is all around them, and that good examples do little good for anyone; never mind that human beings too are mutable, and that much remains for aging lovers to discover about one another: the passions of old age in their own way are as strong and full of revelations as those of youth.

For a modern feminist reader, there's something perverse about all this glorification of self-sacrifice (and maybe Schmitt's breakdown suggests that, at some level, she'd concur). Why can't Ellie have love and art too? Why can't Julianne and Albrecht slip quietly away from lives that have given them nothing but torment to a quiet life together? Clearly such outcomes would do violence to fates and characteristics conventionally assigned to women, to that set of virtues which, until recently, has been assumed to be as much a part of a woman's genetic endowment as breasts and vagina. But there is more than this. In particular, there is the deep connection between love and art.

Why do writers write? Joan Didion says it's an act of aggression, a forcing of oneself into the space of another. It surely is that. But what do we want when we get there? We bring with us our artifacts, the concrete expression of our inner lives, our spirits; and having forced ourselves into a stranger's space, *we hope for nothing less than love.* Schmitt herself willingly admitted this, as Peggy Knapp's essay informs us, and speaking for myself and every other writer I've known, Gladys Schmitt is typical. Moreover, the mindless hero worship any published writer encounters for the mere fact of having been in print won't do in this case. What we want is an admiring love—ah, how clever, how honest, how noble, how perceptive, how affecting, how marvelous you are! We want praise not only for the content of our disclosures, but for the form they take as well. We are voracious. (I've heard research scientists say the same thing; such hunger is hardly limited to artists.)

What makes the appetite more acute with women writers is the way women are socialized to value love above everything, in particular, the love of men for them. It's human to crave love, but most women and most artists are downright addicts. There grows in women writers a nearly unbearable tension between wanting to please and be loved as women—thereby conforming to that extreme set of values such as spirituality, pity, submission, humility, and self-sacrifice, not to mention current ideas of comeliness—and wanting to achieve as writers, which takes courage to test the flesh, a clear-eyed view, unfettered autonomy, not a little arrogance, and a sense of self-fulfillment. Under those circumstances, love can be elusive.

The parallel themes of Schmitt's first and last novels testify that these tensions between wanting to be loved, though it means self-sacrifice, and wanting to achieve as an artist haunted her all her life. In the early part of *The Gates of Aulis,* Ellie senses she can have art or love, but not both. Yet *Aulis* ends by rejecting sacrifice as a way of life, affirms that the human experience must comprise tastes —no, great gulps—of both extremes; that balance, in the end, is best. Carl finally discovers that flesh can be good for you. Ellie's paintings are declared to be of the world, instead of pulling viewers away from it.

Referring to her own paintings, Ellie says: "These reckon with the world and accept the world. I used to think that only one thing was of any consequence: the minute when the absolute self emerges from the swathings of circumstance, naked, classless, habitless, with no attributes except the essential ones—*desire and pity and wounds and a foreknowledge of death.* I told myself the rest was nothing but externals; I said I would go naked to meet the essential nakedness; I said I could dispense with the rest. But that was a fallacy. Such naked dealings are possible only with the dying who have already turned their backs on the works and habits of their ordinary days, who have already begun to forego the world. With the living, it's another matter. No living person is ever so naked as that. The world is not our clothes upon our bodies; the world is an intrinsic part of us. To discount a man's days, to reckon only with his absolute self, to consider nothing but the bare, high hour that comes once in a thousand nights—that is to live only half a life, and half a life is not enough, not for me and not for Eugene. To paint the ultimate self without the world is to paint the truth, yes, but only half a truth, only truth's skeleton. I won't be doing that any more" (642).

Ellie says this, but the conflicts continued to haunt Schmitt. What strikes me about *The Godforgotten* is that all those odd social arrangements in St. Cyprian's—nuns and monks married and begetting, peasants raised up to the aristocracy and lords sent out to the fields, a world turned topsy-turvy—do *not* include any different arrangements at all for the two sexes. This surprised me when I read it, for it was 1972 and feminism was crackling in the air, and had been during the years that Schmitt was at work on the novel. It certainly wasn't that Schmitt evaded the trendy. The scenes of ergot poisoning are a deliberate, conscious response to the psychedelic fancies of the late sixties and early seventies. If she felt moved to comment on altered states of consciousness (all rather negatively, as it happens) why had she evaded making a much more significant statement about the roles of men and women? How could this otherwise brilliant book have failed to take advantage of the opportunity to explore a different, perhaps more balanced, kind of relationship between men and women from the one that, as these essays show, bedeviled Schmitt all her life?

I don't know and now I must speculate, my only evidence being the books themselves, the recollections of her friends who knew her much better than I ever did, and my own experience as woman and writer.

We write as an act of aggression, but such a muted act. We don't press our books on people; we're slightly embarrassed to talk about them. We write to discover ourselves and the meaning of our lives, but with the intention of disclosing that self and meaning to others, to earn their love. We write, in short, for an audience. And we're very finely tuned to certain members of it, who are of course the people who matter most to us, our families, our dear friends, our lovers. We write them messages sometimes so elegantly disguised that they hardly recognize they are being addressed. Here's where we avenge ourselves on a father we could never defy in real life, where we murmur love to a forbidden lover, sympathy to a mother whose situation we have only now come to understand. But most of all, I think, we're sensitive to our mates, those men or women to whom we've made a formal commitment.

When the writer is a woman and her mate is a husband, we are bringing not only the sensibilities of two individuals to bear, but the instruction of an entire society in what is appropriate for women's behavior with men. Thus Norman Mailer, say, can write page after page of the most misogynistic prose fiction imaginable, and not an eyebrow is raised for years among critics, readers, or, one supposes, his wives. When Mailer was writing *An American Dream,* it was an unquestioned part of the common culture to despise women, for women were thought to be despicable. But it has never been part of the common culture to despise men, and the woman writer who discloses some of the reasons she finds men despicable is in serious jeopardy of first, finding no publisher, since the publishing industry is highly patriarchal, and second, offending some specific man in her life who has not been accustomed, let alone numbed, to the idea of seeing his gender systematically vilified in print. A woman who goes farther and suggests other ways for women to be—autonomous, self-fulfilled, self-loving—is really looking for trouble.

There's psychological but not necessarily real-world logic involved here. Those circumstances which have traditionally kept women subordinate to men—men's greater physical strength, their economic and political power—may not necessarily be operational in any individual case, but the habit is nearly impossible to overcome. So it is that Susan Braudy, a journalist, goes to interview Joan Didion for an article in a feminist magazine and finds Didion's husband answering all the questions—Didion herself is "too shy." So it is that Gladys Schmitt was the major wage earner, and often the sole one, between her and Simon Goldfield, and still, at some level, drew back from giving offense. Lois Fowler's essay on the Schmitt-Goldfield marriage suggests some complicated reasons for that, and other essays talk about Schmitt's problematical relationship with her father.

Still, as readers we're left to ask—in mourning and in anger on Schmitt's behalf, rather than puzzlement—what kind of massive offense it would have been to the men who mattered in Schmitt's life, ghosts and flesh alike, if she had exercised her splendid imagination to its fullest and really given us a world where patriarchal retribution had disapeared, where everyone behaved as if she or he were genuinely forgotten by that quintessential patriarch, the God of the Israelites? Would Julianne still have found it necessary to be flirtatious and cajoling to persuade her husband? Would she have felt compelled to choose compassion over desire? Or rather, why not compassion for herself for a change?

I am saying here that it was not so much a failure of imagination as a failure of will that accounts for this startling evasion of the chance to explore a different kind of relationship between men and women. Reconsider Julianne's last reason for renouncing Albrecht: "What we have had of each other was a ripeness. There is a night at harvest time when the fruit on the bough is perfect—sound of skin and sweet in to the stone, and with the coming of another night, it is not more, but less. We have been fortunate in that we harvested in the ultimate hour. What could we desire that we have not been given? What could be revealed to us that we do not know?"

But that's only half the truth, the young Gladys Schmitt would have protested; the other half has to do with the world, with living and growing old, and discovering not only the night in a thousand but the thousand nights. The self-abnegating extremes to which women might be pushed were an outrage for the young Schmitt. But the old and sick Schmitt, writing after years of struggle, had yielded, had tragically come round to her own character's definition thirty years before of "the dying who have already turned their backs on the works and habits of their ordinary days, who have already begun to forego the world."

The struggle Gladys Schmitt endured, described in these essays, is two-fold. On the eastern front is the artist's struggle, a human one, to grasp at truth and love. Engaged in art, any artist accepts the risk that despite one's best efforts, truth, or love, may be impossible. That struggle is difficult enough.

But Schmitt fought on the western front as well, and her adversary was the role she was expected to play as female in a society with strict regulations about such behavior and ruthless penalities for violation. Her struggle with that adversary took many forms, and gallant they were, as these essays attest. Did her university reject the young Schmitt because she was, she saw, too candid? She went on to write her much-praised first novel. Did she fail to conform to conventional standards of female beauty? She wrote beautiful prose instead. Did the hand of a husband rest with indecent weight upon her literary style, not to mention her life? Then Schmitt found another way to release the playfulness and childlike energy she was denied in her writing, and poured it into friendships, students, and needlework instead.

But how long can anyone, whatever her strength and gifts, wage war on two fronts? Schmitt's stepdaughter Elizabeth Culley observes that *The Godforgotten* was written with resignation, with knowledge known too late. Where thirty years earlier, Ellie at the end of *The Gates of Aulis* finally understands that, for the artist, one extreme must balance the other, thereby making a rich middle way, on the contrary, Julianne of *The Godforgotten* renounces, resigns herself (a telling phrase) without protest. No wonder. For the writer, thirty years of non-stop war had intervened.

Schmitt had been fighting a battle all women writers fight, and she had sensed it from the very beginning. It is for the right to be known, accepted—and loved—as we are, not as men would have us be. If women's writing is self-definition, it cannot be edited by husbands, lovers, department chairmen, publishers, or critics, to conform to patriarchal notions of proper womanhood and still be authentic. It is then something else. Its lack of authenticity swindles us all, whether we're the writers who dissimulate because our authentic selves are judged unlovable, or we're the readers who long for a better correspondence in fiction with the richness and variation of our own experience as real women and men.

I am angry at such a terrible summation. It is anger not at the artist, but on her behalf. If there's failure of will rather than imagination in *The Godforgotten* (for Schmitt's imagination seldom failed her), every word in these essays tells us the tragic reasons why. If Schmitt had finally, in Ellie's words, settled for truth's skeleton instead of truth, her spiritual fatigue must be inevitable after such a massive, double-fronted battle. The wonder is that she fought as hard, as elegantly, and as enduringly as she did. Schmitt was an individual, who lived her life as she must, in complex, unique ways.

But she also suffered, and surely her art was hobbled, in ways many women have come to identify as common in our society, and no longer tolerable. These were part of her works and days, and I read Ellie's final declaration as a prescient benediction for us, to see Schmitt in the works and habits and circumstances of her world, the better to understand her absolute self.

We understand and we are angry. In our anger on her behalf, in our compassion for her spiritual fatigue, a fatigue which has impoverished us all, we are justified in grieving our loss.

THE PATTERN IN THE TAPESTRY

Dorothy Rosenberg

I never knew Gladys in the classroom. I never heard her give a public lecture. I know her best through the romance of her novels, the agonies of her sonnets—and through our personal friendship, her need to give herself to her friends in a one to one relationship, her self-effacement as a woman, her sense of helplessness in a world almost too ugly for her to bear. I think of her as a woman with much more of her personality locked in and controlled than ever found its way into her writing or her social life. And I think it was her stitchery that helped her cope with a world that took too much of her, while stitchery also gave her a medium to express what was otherwise subdued.

Alfred Lord Tennyson describes my image of Gladys better than I ever could in his lyric poem *The Lady of Shalott*. The story—it's a beautiful fantasy—is this: a lady has embowered herself in a castle tower because she has been told that if she so much as looks upon the world, something terrible will happen to her. "She knows not what the curse may be." She longs for life, and so she hangs a mirror in front of her window on which "the shadows of the world appear." And she "Weaves the mirror's magic sights" into her tapestry. One day Sir Lancelot blazes into her glass on his "gemmy-bridled" war-horse, his golden shield shining among the lilies along the river, his coalblack curls flowing beneath his helmet.

> She left the web, she left the loom,
> She made three paces through the room,
> She saw the water lily bloom,
> She saw the helmet and the plume,
>   She looked down on Camelot.
> Out flew the web and floated wide;
> The mirror cracked from side to side;
> "The curse has come upon me," cried
>   The Lady of Shalott.

Dorothy Rosenberg has been an actress (winter stock) in Boston and Lowell, Mass-achusetts, and has taught acting and English. More recently, she taught stitchery while working at a local yarn shop.

She came down from her sheltered tower, found a boat along the river bank, wrote her name round about the prow of it, loosed her snowy-white robes, laid down in the boat and floated down the river singing her last song as she died.

Perhaps Tennyson was talking about the artist. Perhaps he was saying that it is inherent in the artist's nature to be unable to involve himself with life, to deal directly with it—that to save his life he must live it vicariously, see it reflected in a glass in order to objectify it. Perhaps Tennyson was talking, as well, about women—about what we now think of as women's conditioning. For girls have traditionally been taught to be delicate, attractive, fuzzyheaded, refined, domestic, unaggressive, nurturing. When such a woman reaches her maturity—almost a contradiction in terms—she's not trained to distinguish between illusion and reality. And so she lives a largely illusory life until faced with the curse of reality. Of course, women don't all immediately drop dead when this happens, but often they suffer the loss of illusion before they feel the gain of reality; and since all things are relative, many of them never experience the gain.

All this, in my opinion, with only a slightly different twist, is what happened to Gladys. She looked down upon the world more often than the Lady of Shalott, and her curse was more slowly lethal. As Gladys was an artist, she needed to retreat from life in order to objectify it. As she was a woman, she needed to maintain the illusions of femininity. More so because she was a woman living in what is still largely a man's world. And she was a homely woman. And she was an undomestic woman. And she was a childless woman. And burning through all of the intellectuality was a woman's heart and a woman's ego—her woman's conditioning.

Certainly one of the most compassionate people I have ever known, Gladys was also one of the most defenseless. It didn't matter what her problems were, she was always ready to give her full interest and attention to someone else. A couple on the verge of divorce, a student in trouble with parents, parents in agony over a child's rebellion—these people she devoted herself to regardless of pain or loss of her own. And although it was Gladys' nature to give of herself, it is also human nature to take too much, and I think very often the well was drunk dry and not replenished. Her reputation as a writer was some protection. There are some people who won't tread on hallowed ground. And her scathing sense of humor probably held some at arm's length, although I never knew her to use that aspect of her humor to directly hurt another human being. Stitchery gave her another kind of protection from over-involvement.

In stitchery, too, Gladys found an escape from the editorial hand of her husband, Simon. His taste in art—that is, music and literature —was narrowly classical, with little understanding of or patience with the modern. And his standards were strict. He was not an artist. He was an astute critic—an almost totally intellectual man. These qualities in Simon, I am sure, had great influence on Gladys' fiction. If I were asked to criticize her writing, I would say it lacked fantasy and humor, the two qualities that were very much alive in her personality. I have always felt that it was Simon's watchful and critical eye and old-fashioned approach that either rubbed them out of her writing or caused them to be only lightly used. Simon's mind glittered and Gladys' glowed: it's the glow I miss most in her writing.

Much of what was expressed in Gladys' needlework was this fantasy and humor, as well as the womanliness that was largely cut off in her professional life. Here was a domestic act, and she performed it without irony, without fear or striving, working intuitively. She told me once that it was sheer sensual abandon to spend lots of money on the slippery, glowing colors that went into her needlework.

Indeed, needlework is an occupation of the senses rather than of the intellect. Design, color, texture, taction all come together in the hands to make a lovely and practical object. It is an act which, if done reasonably well, can only be admired. This is particularly true if, as it was for Gladys, it is a secondary art. If you stitch in a room full of guests, which Gladys often did, you can be as gracious as you choose to be, and if a subject is introduced which you don't care to pursue, you can hold up your piece and say, "Shall I put blue here, in this little spot, or grey?" And the world is held at bay until you are mended and soothed and ready to say, as the Lady of Shalott did, "I am half sick of shadows," and come out to test your strength against the next onslaught.

Gladys' stitchery fulfilled artistic needs, too; it was extraordinarily good. She did all of her own designing and worked in two motifs exclusively, as far as I know. One was the medieval crowns, castles, mythological monsters, dragons, old lettering; and the other was all of nature's creatures—flowers, birds, animals.

One piece I remember vividly is stitched on black linen about ten inches wide and twenty-four inches long. Three twiggy, leaf-less branches embroidered in brown wool come from the left and are evenly spaced down the length of the cloth. Perched on each branch is an owl; all three are alike, and so beautifully sewn in greys and whites, with such creative use of the stitches, that you can feel them wrapped and snuggled in their feathers, ruffled and sleepy-eyed against the cold. White snowflakes dot the background. When I worked in a needlepoint shop, I hung this piece behind the counter near the door. Hundreds of customers remarked on it, and I could have sold it as many times.

This simple, quiet kind of entity was her specialty. Each piece was like a poem—complete, contained within itself, to move you as you would be moved; and there was nothing more to ask of it. And there was often in these creature pieces a sense of suspended animation, of isolation—each creature was set in relationship only to a replica of itself—a suspended repeat pattern, delightful to the eye, calming to the senses.

Gladys herself describes such a piece of stitchery in her last novel, *The Godforgotten*. The piece was made by a character who is herself a telling portrait of a giving woman: the ragged, bedraggled, yet essentially feminine whore Jehanne, who gives her body to all men who want it out of compassion for their need. Jehanne presents the piece to Father Albrecht, the representative of the Church, as a gift of love. He is unhappy about accepting it from her; he con-demns her not only for her carnality, but for stealing the thread she used to make the stitchery. Yet even he has to admire its surpassing beauty:

> What she unrolled and laid across his knees was a piece of stitchery like nothing he had ever seen before. On a dun colored strip of cloth the length of an arm and the width of a hand, three sea gulls des-cended, one beneath the other, in swirls of snow. The design exalted nature without elaborating it or imposing upon it, and the workman-ship put to shame the arras of the Deadly Sins and the Cardinal Virtues that was the glory of Cologne. The entirety asserted itself only in a kind of whisper: white, grey, darker grey and black on a quiet background of dun—the one real color was in the little knots of scarlet set like jewels in the six red eyes and the six red feet"
> (p. 186).

The medieval subject matter in some of Gladys' stitchery reflects a lifelong interest and is, of course, closely connected with her writing. Although the stitchery was privately her own in its execu-tion, it was not a thing totally apart from her professional life. While she was working on *The Godforgotten,* she created one of her most memorable pieces, the sunken cathedral. The stitchery was done mostly in greys and blues, in tones and stitches that gave the illusion of looking through a deep and gently washing water. It was in the medieval patterns—the things of the past—where the color and drama flowed. Vibrant, bejewelled crowns, castles, and shields with crests were geometrically arranged with a flawless sense of balance and design.

Probably her most impressive achievement, at least in scope, is finally the alphabet series she designed shortly before her death. She had made a pair of pillows for a friend with the letters H and L. She loved the integral self-containment of the form and decided to do a complete alphabet. Each colorful letter is sewn on a twelve inch piece of linen, each with a design suggested by the shape of the letter. The B became a castle, the J a Viking ship; she used musical motifs, bees, flowers, snails, anything that worked.

Over the years, her work did undergo a change. The earlier pieces were like Jehanne's in *The Godforgotten*—delicate, monochromatic, quiet. Small creatures were stitched on small pieces of cloth; the effect was like a fine doily. But after the troubles of the late 1950's and '60's—the frustration over the meager critical and popular reception of *Rembrandt,* the deaths of family members and friends, Simon's breakdown and her own—the stitchery picked up action and a flamboyant humor it hadn't had before. I'm thinking here of two pieces, companion pieces, of monkeys in a tree top, jumping and noisy. There are big leaves of bright greens and yellows in the scene, and the mischievous, lively monkeys, done in turkey tuft stitch, are about to leap off the trees into your hands. There had been a turnabout. The fight and defiance had gone out of her life and to some extent out of her fictional characters. But here it was—expressed in her stitchery.

Also, in the last years, her attitude toward this second art changed. I discovered this at the Goldfields' house one evening, not many months before her death. She was sewing a bright red cardinal on a piece of black linen. He was sitting on a brown, snow-patched branch. She finished it before the evening was over, displayed it proudly to everyone, as she always did, and put it aside. She opened the little stand by her chair, pulled out another piece of cloth stamped with another pattern and began a new piece. I was surprised and asked her if she didn't take a count and a half between pieces. She laughed and said she was always more than a count and a half ahead of herself and impatient to finish the last so she could begin the next. She told me that night that she had become so absorbed in the needlework that she was almost tempted to quit teaching and devote all of her time to it. She said it with apology and a touch of defiance. We didn't pursue the subject but were led by others in the room into a debate of the merits of Jane Austen's prose.

Later, when I explored that remark, I discovered that she was deep into planning the marketing of her designs. She was going to kit them in plastic bags with a pattern stamped on linen and enough wool to complete the stitching. She was mentally planning formats for books to teach the stitches and textures. She had all but contracted for a show of her work in Washington, D.C. She was about to embark on another career, which I'm certain would have been successful.

There is, by the way, one last ironic correspondence between the writing and the stitchery that I can't help but note—that the public recognition and achievement she looked for finally eluded her. Gladys died before the business plans could be accomplished and before she could complete negotiations for the show in Washington. A show of her stitchery was mounted in Pittsburgh, at the Old Post Office Museum; but that was after her death. Most of her work is dispersed now—scattered among her relatives and friends who value it, I'm sure, for its artistry and beauty, and even more for its expression of Gladys' friendship and of her need to give—but most of all because its creation was a joy to her, joy experienced in the doing and joy expressed in the product as it was nowhere else so fully expressed.

Sister Dorothy, brother Bob, father Henry, and Gladys—about 1914.

Gladys' mother Leonore and
her maternal grandmother.

Gladys and sister Dorothy—about 1914.

Family portrait:
brother Bob, Gladys,
sister Dorothy,
and mother Leonore—
mid 1920's.

Gladys' aunt Ollie and her niece Betty
(Bob's daughter)—late 1930's.

Simon (left) and Gladys, watching the typesetting of *David the King*—published
by Dial Press, 1946.

Dust jacket photograph for *Rembrandt*—published 1961.

Gladys in the late 1960's.

THE HISTORICAL NOVEL

Jan Cohn

Gladys Schmitt's novels have customarily been divided into two types, those set in the contemporary world and those cast in a more remote historical period. It has been customary as well to judge the two sets of novels differently: to find the relatively shorter stories of contemporary life sensitive, subtle, but finally failed; to find the longer and more lavish novels set in the past, grand, profound, distinguished. It was with *David the King* (1946) that Schmitt first achieved real success; and subsequently, *Confessors of the Name* (1952) and, particularly, *Rembrandt* (1961) received serious critical approval. By the time that *Rembrandt* was published, the two-part classification of Schmitt's novels seemed clear enough. Furthermore, her reputation was seen as resting on the achievement of what Edmund Fuller called "the three big books that are not modern in setting."[1]

Fuller's phrasing is cautious. "Books that are not modern in setting" is a roundabout way of saying "historical novels," but the idea of the historical novel is a troublesome one for a critic dealing with a serious novel. In fact, the historical novel has been for at least a century a vehicle for popular entertainment, seldom a form selected for serious, philosophical fiction. As Roger Sale put it, "It may well be that an almost sure formula for remaining unknown is to write a serious historical novel."[2] Still, Gladys Schmitt elected three times to take her chances against this "sure formula," to commit her energy and seriousness to a form well established as a vehicle for popular entertainment.

The historical novel was not, of course, always demeaned as merely entertainment. Early in the nineteenth century, Sir Walter

Jan Cohn is Associate Professor and Director of Graduate Studies in English at Carnegie-Mellon University. Her principal areas of teaching and research are American literature and society, and the related field of popular literature. Her published articles include studies of American literary realism, the American house as a cultural symbol, and the early responses to the Civil War in magazine fiction. She is currently completing work on a biography of Mary Roberts Rinehart.

Scott attracted a wide and varied audience. The vogue of *Ivanhoe* and *The Bride of Lammermoor* was enormous, reaching a public that excluded only that "moral elite" still waging war against the novel in any guise. But between the time of Scott and that of Gladys Schmitt much had changed in the conception of the novel. Most important in that change were two developments in literary history, the movement toward realism and the development of *avant garde* art.

Realism has been the subject of hundreds of definitions and descriptions, and there is no need to recapitulate them here. However, it is important to note that realism implies, if it does not demand, a focus on the present. Ian Watt, in his history of the novel, talks specifically of the way in which writers of novels turned away from traditional story materials and constructed their plots out of original and especially contemporary materials.[3] Certainly by 1900 serious American fiction was dominated by realistic writers who turned to the world of the cities, of business, of competitive American society and to the problems and issues facing contemporary men and women in that society. Not only the novels, but the essays and letters of William Dean Howells, Frank Norris, Theodore Dreiser emphasize the significance of a realistic treatment of modern life, suggesting that other subjects, other focuses, represented an evasion of the novelist's responsibility.

Not that the reading public was necessarily imbued with a similar sense of responsibility. Any survey of best-sellers in America, from the end of the nineteenth century to the present day, indicates how important escape literature has been. The sentimental romances and dime novels of the last century, the detective stories and science fiction of our time, have sold more successfully than the serious novels of Dreiser or Howells, of Pyncheon or Bellow. Among best-selling fiction in the twentieth century have been a good number of historical novels, novels without much claim to seriousness of purpose but with demonstrable entertainment value. Irving Stone and Frank Yerby, for example, brought the historical novel to a wide audience and in doing so contributed to the definition of the function and the quality of that kind of popular fiction.

The distinction between popular and elite fiction, a clear enough distinction in the latter part of the nineteenth century, was sharpened in the twentieth with the work of artists who surrendered any hope of even moderate popular success by the complexity of their work. *The avant garde* art of the modern period fostered an elitist and inward-looking attitude in the writer, as it did in the painter and musician of the period. Cut off from the larger public, thrown more and more upon the values and judgments of a small circle of fellow-artists, the modern writer produced works of great technical virtuosity. The reader was left to find his own way through the later novels of Henry James, or the works of Conrad, Joyce, and Faulkner. Relatively few readers possessed the requisite sophistication.

The serious writers of the modern period did not ignore the past, but they used it in new ways, in ways absolutely distinct from those employed by writers of historical novels. The classical and medieval world appears in the novels of James Joyce or the poems of T. S. Eliot in fragments, in references, in analogies available only to the most highly educated. This is no rich recreation of time and place in which the reader may lose himself, but a compendium of learning meant to enrich the intellectual texture of the work—for those who were up to it. Emerson had said that "To be great is to be misunderstood"; it must have seemed to a baffled reading public that the *avant garde,* elite artist now insisted that to be great was not to be understood at all. To that end, the serious novelist avoided the materials and the forms that seemed to belong to the popular novelist.

The historical novel, the "costume romance," was a form to be avoided. The sentimental and swashbuckling fictions that had changed little from the weak imitations of the novels of Sir Walter Scott attracted their own reading public; it was not an intellectual audience. By the middle of the twentieth century, moreover, the historical romance, essentially unaffected by literary realism and radically separated from the serious fiction of elite artists, was further debased by two additional developments. For one thing, changing social mores, a loosening of censorship in fiction, brought more overt sex to the historical novel. *Forever Amber,* bringing together the terrors of the plague and the titillations of the bedroom in seventeenth century England, was a success.

A second influence on the historical novel was the exploitation of historical materials in blockbuster movies, especially the Biblical dramas of Cecil B. DeMille. Any subtleties of character delineation or refinements of philosophical speculation that might have existed in a novel like Lloyd Douglas's *The Robe* were certainly lost in its translation to the screen. Hollywood, in working the rich vein of Biblical stories, reinforced the connection between historical fiction and spectacle. Similar in the dependence on color and action and on the minimization of character and theme were Hollywood's popularizations of the life-stories of artists, writers, and musicians of the past. Again, spectacle and sentiment were foremost, and again, historical fiction—in this case in a quasi-biographical mode—was debased.

It was in this environment that Gladys Schmitt conceived *David the King, Confessors of the Name,* and *Rembrandt,* all three in forms that Hollywood had exploited—the Biblical narrative, the story of Christian martyrdom in Imperial Rome, and the biography of the great artist. There is, then, a striking irony in the discontinuity between form and substance in Schmitt's three big novels, for the subject-matter with which she chose to deal was subject-matter intimately connected with spectacle and sentimentality. But Gladys Schmitt had neither a swashbuckling imagination nor a sentimental intellect; she turned to these subjects and to the form of the historical novel with very different skills and strengths and for very different purposes. Her big novels do not fit the popular expectations for the genre she chose.

David the King was Schmitt's most successful novel. Here the form of the historical novel, the subject-matter, the texture, and the characterizations came together in her most satisfactory fusion of a popular form with a more serious purpose. For the serious reader of novels, *David the King* provided both richly drawn characters and philosophical weight. Furthermore, as in all Schmitt's novels, the language is highly wrought, consciously "artistic." For the less sophisticated reader, the story had its own rewards, rewards that lay partly in the story itself and partly in Schmitt's working out of the actions and their causes.

A Biblical narrative, like the retelling of any well-known tale, depends less on the construction of a story-line than on the filling in of detail and the working out of psychological motivations for anticipated actions. Schmitt's creative imagination was often struck by the most fragmentary of information. For *David,* the Biblical story with its salient events and cryptic commentaries left a great deal for the novelistic imagination. *Rembrandt,* too, was constructed from very sparse biographical data. General historical research provided Schmitt the material out of which she wove the texture of her novels—the houses, clothing, food, manners. The inner qualities of the characters, however, she drew without sources other than those that her life and her observations of other people, and herself, provided her. In *David the King* research and observation made ancient Israel a dense and almost tactile landscape and filled that land with complex and believable studies of familiar characters —David, Saul, Jonathan, Absalom.

For all the brilliance in *David,* there are faults as well, and these are faults common to all three of the big novels. The book is very long and its length is due in part to a tendency to draw episodes out too long and in part to a fascination with psychologizing that goes on too far. There are, as well, places where the action comes to a stop, providing spaces in which the speculative, philosophical passages may occur. *David,* by its very nature, allows for a good deal of speculation, for the history of King David is rich in moments that call for the deepest questions about human life, human relationships, and the relation of men to God. Still, philosophizing does not always sit comfortably with the more active, even action-filled, quality of the novel. Finally, the language of *David the King,* for all its richness and elegance, seems at times too careful, too self-consciously "fine," and in itself creates some sense of disjunction between the novel as story and the novel as "writing." Although one cannot be sure, it appears as though the very fineness of the language were a defense against the more popular and sensational qualities of the historical novel.

Confessors of the Name is the least of the big three, lacking the appeal that brought *David the King* to a wide audience and the scope and weight that gave *Rembrandt* its critical significance. *Confessors* is set in Imperial Rome and it tells the story of Imperial intrigue, Roman aristocratic life, and Christian martyrdom. The details in the novel bring the reader into intimate connection with life under the Emperor Decius. Schmitt depicts the Imperial court, the Emperor amid counselors and flatterers. Of aristocratic life we have the urban house, the streets and shops, the country villa. We enter the world of the poor as well, in Roman tenements and in the prison where the Christians await their final journey to the Colosseum.

The story is complex, bringing together political considerations and philosophical-religious points of view in a plot that involves both love and martyrdom. While Schmitt writes what are perhaps her most active dramatic scenes in this novel, she never comes close to sensationalism, somehow keeping even so similar a story clear of the blur and racket of the chariot race in *Ben Hur.* The scenes in which the martyrs are moved from their prison to the Colisseum and the climactic episode in which these martyrs, including Paulina, the heroine of the novel, move forward to the waiting horror of the lions in the arena are filled with terror, but with dignity as well.

Confessors has some of the strengths and all of the weaknesses of *David*. Again, the novel often seems too long, too ponderous; there is often too much insistence on the high moral seriousness of the characters, on the commitment of Paulina and of Favorinus, the novel's hero, to belief, to meaning, to renunciation. The intellectual aspect of the novel is more complex than in *David*; the debates on the relative merits of Stoicism versus Christianity do not always fit with the more novelistic aspects of *Confessors*. Furthermore, the novel is darker than *David*, partly because the major characters do not share with King David the triumphs and excitements of a long and event-filled life. To some extent, though, the novel is more brooding, more filled with a sense of the tragic, as a reflection of Schmitt's own life, her own questions about love and work and belief. Finally, while *Confessors* impresses with its rich complexity and sustained seriousness, it fails ever to come fully to life with the intensity of the finest fiction. It is a cool book, too controlled, again too self-consciously fine. Even Edmund Fuller, always a critic friendly to Schmitt, thought it missed the "peak" Schmitt was capable of attaining, but he labeled the novel "distinguished."[4] Another critic aptly expressed his mixed response, calling it the work of an epic poet in the world of fiction.[5]

Of the three big books, *Rembrandt* is the most sombre. At heart it is a philosophical study of the function and the meaning of art in bourgeois society. Rembrandt van Rijn, as Schmitt sees him, is the provincial come to the city to succeed as an artist, but a man with a family as well, and with the consequent need to attract commissions. The genius, painting differently from the popular artists of his day and driven to discover more and more about mankind, himself, and his own genius through his art, suffers the artistic expectations of seventeenth century Amsterdam; his vision is distinct. As Schmitt constructs the novel, the philosophical questions become the rack on which Rembrandt is tortured. His conflicts and torments make up the psychological stuff of the novel.

Rembrandt is not an unrelievedly sombre book, for as in the other big novels the reader is given generous recreations of life in the Netherlands in Rembrandt's time—of the guilds, the studios, the pancake houses. Nevertheless, to the extent that the novel is a study of the artist, it is a heavy and brooding book. Rembrandt is himself seen as almost constantly in conflict, often in torment. In many ways, he is depicted as the absolute Romantic artist for, without being in the least Byronic, he is always in a posture of antagonism with his society and almost always creating out of struggle or despair, never out of joy. It is tempting to see in *Rembrandt* Schmitt's portrait of herself as an artist, and there are compelling reasons to do so. Certainly, an analogy can be drawn between Rembrandt trying to support himself by infusing into the popular and profitable form of the guild portrait his own unique vision—as in "The Anatomy Lesson" and "The Night Watch"—and Schmitt's own attempt to make the historical novel a vehicle for her complex vision of life. As other chapters in this book explain, the years in which she worked on *Rembrandt* were in many ways terrible years in her personal life and her writing was carried on through a number of seriously traumatic episodes. A good deal of *Rembrandt,* then, reflects Schmitt's own experiences in these years, torn between the demands made on her by her art and by her life and crucified at times by each.

Like the other big books, *Rembrandt* reflects major preoccupations of Schmitt's. These preoccupations are profound moral questions about the nature of life, the value of art, the meaning of life, the terror or promise of death—difficult questions, unanswerable dilemmas. Moreover, the painful answers (and the narrow physical pleasures) Schmitt provides her protagonists seem particularly niggardly when sketched onto such broad, rich canvasses.

Religion is one such constant preoccupation in these novels, even when, as in *Rembrandt,* it is not an essential part of the story-line. It is not, however, conventional religious observances or beliefs that are central; rather, Schmitt remains concerned with a life in some way connected with the idea of God, a life made significant through commitment, and sacrifice, to something of higher value. The moral weight in these novels comes with the notion of commitment and of sacrifice as it is made by men and women of large gifts. For David it is the idea of the Hebrew nation; for Favorinus and Paulina, some notion of the "Name"; for Rembrandt, the idea of art. In every case, and despite what might be seen as of value, great sacrifice is required. Furthermore, in *Confessors* and *Rembrandt* the expectation of sacrifice, the readiness to sacrifice, imbues the whole novel. One lives to be ready for the great renunciation; meanwhile, one gives up a good many homely comforts and sensual pleasures along the way.

Sacrifice is often figured in these novels through the absence of physical desires or the surrender of physical pleasures, usually particularized in eating and in sexuality. There are frequent descriptions of food, associated with richly drawn scenes that serve both to enhance the landscape of each novel and to provide an environment in which characters meet, talk, and make discoveries about themselves and their values. We enter Roman cookshops and Dutch pancake houses and in these places there is real food, specific to its time and place. But the food prepared and set before Schmitt's characters is often unattractive, even repulsive.

At a banquet given by a courtesan in *Confessors* the exotic food becomes foul in the eyes of Favorinus. He sees a slave "bearing a silver tray with a great scaly fish on it," and later on the tray reappears "heaped with fatty slices of suckling pig." Nearby an old poet eats. "A withered hand came up toward the mouth, carrying a piece of fish on a shovel of bread; but the bread fell from the shaking hand onto the silver plate, and the fish splashed into the goblet of wine." More and more food appears. The details are sharp—mussels arrive with a garnish of parsley—but the apparently lush grows rotten. Favorinus thinks of the diners as already "clogged" with food.[6] Favorinus, sated in advance of eating, is sickened by the gross materiality of food as he is sickened by the gross materiality of Rome. His lack of appetite images his possibilities for moral growth.

Gladys Schmitt, often herself revolted by food, yet frequently the hostess at dinner parties for her friends, wrote in *Sonnets for an Analyst:*

> This is a migraine (may you never know).
> The candles on the table jerk and glare.
> The guests are chirping waxworks with false hair;
> Their artificial teeth chop row on row.
> Then comes the nausea, then comes the pain.
> Hideous to have eaten: what's inside—
> Fish, flesh, or fowl—is something that has died
> And yet to spew it up would split the brain.
> The jiggling aura, silver, blue, and red,
> Unstrings, benumbs, takes sight and thought away.
> I drop my clattering fork. I think I say
> "When do you sail?" or was it "Oh, my head?"
> Rotting alive, I manage not to moan.
> But, Christ, I envy rotting wood, dumb windworn stone.

Schmitt's noble characters, king, aristocrat, or artist, do not eat with lust.

Sacrifice is expressed as well through the attitudes of Schmitt's major characters toward sex. King David is, of course, lusty; the Biblical source makes this clear. He is, as well, drawn to Jonathan homosexually, a point that Schmitt does not shrink from. But it is not homosexuality that stands as the opposition or alternative to sexual love; rather it is love without sexuality, a subject important both to *Confessors* and *Rembrandt*.

In *Confessors*, Paulina—and eventually Favorinus—renounce the possibility of consummating their love. In one scene Paulina talks of union through the Lord and explains to Favorinus about the "Thousands of women, renouncing things they find it impossible to possess in the flesh . . . [who] console themselves by bringing what they love to God." Favorinus argues for earthly, physical love: "an obsession, a need so desperate, that life would be meaningless, even impossible, if that person were gone." Paulina acknowledges that such love exists but insists that it is made too much of. "It's doomed to be overblown, since it's the single blossom on the stem . . . . Pampered and over-rich as it is, it's sure to sicken in the end."[7] But she admits, as she departs, that she is not yet without desire. Desire is something to be overcome, and love, something to be renounced. Sexuality can, like food, be sacrificed, an index to commitment, but not without a sense of loss permeating those pages in which lovers like Paulina and Favorinus maintain their spirituality.

Finally, each of the three historical novels is concerned with death, a concern that is intensified with each work. The characters know death; they are faced with the deaths of those they care for. They are faced, beyond that, with the knowledge of their own deaths, the need to come to terms with it, even—in the case of Paulina—to walk toward it in the public arena. There is, at times, a yearning for death or, perhaps more accurately, a wish never to have been burdened with life: "I envy rotting wood, dumb windworn stone." Here, again, is the brooding concern about religious questions, in the broadest sense, questions about death as it weaves through life, shapes life, makes life sometimes bearable and sometimes not. For life, physical life, with its bodily pleasures, is filled with pain and, as well, filled with lures to distract us from the commitment we must develop and the sacrifices we must be prepared to make.

Such issues are not the stuff of the conventional historical novel and the importance of these matters to Schmitt's fiction increases that disjunction between the material of her fiction and the form in which she chose to cast that material. The term "historical novel" offended both Schmitt and her husband; they claimed that none of her novels fit that category, and in some ways that claim is correct, for the novels are not sentimental nor are they adventurous escape literature. Nevertheless, the novels are "historical"; they are fictions set in a recreated past.

More important than definition, though, is the fact that Schmitt frequently and seriously turned to this form, and seemed thereby to attempt a persistent escape from the present to the past. The intellectual and artistic energy spent in reconstructing the details of the past and in exploring the psychological and philosophical states of men and women long dead are facts that cannot be ignored in Schmitt's writing. It is interesting to speculate on why she did choose the historical genre.

Perhaps the answer lies in the freedom Schmitt found in removing her imagination to distant times and places. Those who knew Gladys Schmitt recognized in ancient Israel, Imperial Rome, or mercantile Holland men and women who peopled her landscape in industrial Pittsburgh. Especially familiar are the relationships between husband and wife, or between lovers, particularly in regard to questions about sexuality and to the attempts made at justifying non-physical love relationships. Further, those characteristics of her husband, and of others, that Gladys Schmitt found most unattractive and that elicited her most intense resentment were given to characters for whom it was not necessary to feel affection. It would seem that by transporting the relationships, the questions about love, the less-than-lovely attributes of those she was supposed to care about to other places and times, Schmitt was able to expose them to trenchant analysis and, no doubt, to relieve her own gnawing hostilities.

If this speculation tells us something about why Schmitt returned to the historical novel for three of her major works of fiction, it does not solve the essential problems created by that choice of genre. Despite an occasional major work in this form, like Thomas Mann's *Joseph in Egypt*, the historical novel remains essentially an entertainment and has, in recent decades, taken on only a pseudo-seriousness in those works that attempt to recreate Biblical or early Christian life (*The Robe; The Shoes of the Fisherman*). Schmitt brought genuine seriousness to the form, genuine psychological and philosophical weight, elegant and studied language. Nevertheless, these attributes of elite fiction rest uneasily on the structures of the popular form, so that despite the considerable achievement of *David* the *King, Confessors of the Name,* and *Rembrandt,* the novels fail, at last, to serve as adequate vehicles for the richness and darkness of Schmitt's imagination.

To the extent that the historical novel can succeed as serious fiction, it must represent a contemporary issue through the manners and mores of distant people. It must be true and relevant, at one and the same time, to the past it recreates and the present it serves. Only in *The Godforgotten* does Schmitt achieve that double triumph. In the three big novels, it is less the modern world and much more the private world of Gladys Schmitt that is translated into the stories of David, Favorinus and Paulina, and Rembrandt van Rijn. Ironically, this genre seems in the case of the three big novels to have allowed the novelist herself the escape that the historical novel has conventionally promised to its audience.

NOTES

[1]Edmund Fuller, "Gladys Schmitt: 'Jacob and the Angel,' " *American Scholar,* XXXI (Summer, 1961), 412.

[2]Roger Sale, "Unknown Novels," *American Scholar,* XLIII (Winter, 1973), 96.

[3]Ian Watt, *The Rise of the Novel* (Berkeley, Calif: Univ. of California Press, 1965), pp. 13-15.

[4]Edmund Fuller, Review of *Confessors of the Name, Saturday Review of Literature,* XXXV (November 15, 1952), 16.

[5]W. T. Scott, Review of *Confessors of the Name,* New York *Herald Tribune Book Review* (October 26, 1952), p. 1.

[6]Gladys Schmitt, *Confessors of the Name* (New York: Dial Press, 1952), pp. 171-74.

[7]*Ibid.,* pp. 301-06.

FIVE HEROINES: A PERSISTENT IMAGE

Anita Brostoff

If we can accuse Gladys Schmitt of being an "old fashioned" novelist—one who believed, like Henry James, in the necessity and interdependence of character and event as the base of fiction—her work at least deserves recognition for having the virtues of the "old fashioned" novel. Characterization, in fact, was Schmitt's great strength. Whether she started with a historical figure or an imagined one, she put flesh on the bone, contradiction and conflict in the mind, moral complexity in the actions of her characters. How ironic it is, then, that Schmitt's major female characters—sterling heroines all, real and memorable individuals all, women in different times and cultures—turn out to be, essentially, one and the same woman.

The resemblances among them strike you inescapably when you begin to think about it. There are five women to think about, five who are either protagonists or who carry significant supporting roles: Ellie in *The Gates of Aulis*, Alexandra, Paulina in *Confessors of the Name*, Electra, and Julianne in *The Godforgotten*.* The basic similarities are perhaps to be expected: like most 20th century heroines, they are women in search of themselves, of their femininity, of their place and meaning in society. But these crises of identity and role aren't the whole story. The similarities go deeper, into the heroines' specific need to resolve their sexuality and their attempt to deal with this crisis through religion—in a larger sense, myth—or through art. Altogether, the likenesses—and the dif-

*In two historical novels, *David the King* and *Rembrandt*, the male hero dominates the book to the point where no female carries comparable stature. I omit discussion of the heroines of two novels with modern settings, *A Small Fire* and *The Persistent Image*, largely because these novels lack some of the essential features of the more representative works.

Anita Brostoff is Adjunct Assistant Professor and Co-Director of the Communication Skills Center at Carnegie-Mellon University. She has taught all kinds of writing—from fiction to technical writing—at the university and in the community, has trained teachers of writing, and has written articles on Schmitt's Sonnets *for an Analyst.*

ferences—tell/ an interesting tale. Looking at the five heroines in succession, in the order Schmitt created them, you experience not only an image of woman's abiding dilemma and her possibilities for resolution, but also an image of Schmitt's own progression as woman and as artist. For what she sensed but disguised when she wrote her first published novel, she admitted, richly, in her last one.

Not everything about these characters, of course, but many significant details suggest Schmitt's own problems; we can't ignore the parallels. Nor can we fail to note that the common traits, motives, and situations of the heroines are those that work to undermine and destroy a woman. Each of them feels somehow inadequate; each believes she is insufficient as sexual object, wife, lover, even mother (since all are barren). Her sense of her womanhood has been damaged by deprivation of love. In some portrayals we are shown the primal source of the problem: denial of love by the character's parents, particularly the mother, makes the character feel she is unworthy of being loved and unsuited to fill the feminine role as her mother does. More to the point in the novels, however, is the deprivation of love by a husband or lover, a deprivation which reinforces the feelings of unworthiness and unfeminineness. Not surprisingly, these heroines who believe that they can't get love are equally incapable of giving healthy love to a man. Each commits herself to the wrong man—a self-absorbed, withdrawn creature with whom no satisfactory sexual relationship is possible—and feels something more like pity or gratitude than love for him. In each story, the heroine is broken by her committed loyalty to the man who does not love her and whom she does not love.

Add to this personal deprivation the state created by living in a world where the old, objective standards of right and wrong are being questioned, while no clear new standards have arrived. In such a world people must make choices: they must find moral attitudes which will enable them to cope. Schmitt's women (and men, for that matter) never have unambiguously good moral choices. Furthermore, the women lack freedom of choice: for all their courage and intelligence, they are hampered emotionally by their personal, sexual problems and externally by societal precepts which define their role in highly restrictive ways. As a result, even when their chosen resolution contains an affirmation of certain moral values, it denies the possibility of happiness or success for them in their worlds. Each heroine becomes in some sense, either literal or symbolic, suicidal. Schmitt's resolutions for women imply at best ambiguous, uneasy, or bitter acceptance, and at worst, despair.*

The Gates of Aulis (Dial Press: New York, 1942) is in many ways a flawed book. As the reviewers said, there's too much verbiage, too much sensibility. The plot lacks the fullness, and the characters lack the stature, to carry the themes. But the book sets forth the fundamentals of Schmitt's vision. Romanticized, over-described, imperfectly tied together and balanced, all the threads of character and circumstance developed in later books are here.

At twenty-five, the heroine, Ellie Hasselmann, wants to establish her identity as a woman in traditional ways. Schmitt shows us and dismisses the more attractive alternatives. Physical beauty, one way for a woman to gain love, recognition, and power, won't serve. Ellie knows very well that she's too thin, unblossomed, not beautiful. Accomplishment is another way. Ellie is a painter, but in her present emotional state she can't come up to her potential as an artist. Her only other choice, it seems, is to be a giving woman, to try to find self-fulfillment through helping others achieve the fulfillment they need.

Ellie gives herself—literally gives her body—for the sake of love. She seeks recognition through love so desperately because she has been deprived of both and needs to prove she's worthy of them. Her parents are and have always been remote strangers: she thinks of them as "the mother" and "the father," as if they weren't her relatives, but objects or symbols. She feels most keenly deprived of the love of her strongly feminine mother, a being she doesn't know, "one who exists only in relationship to other beings and things— clocks, father, meals, visitors, ironing boards, and unmade beds" (81). Out of this non-relationship arises the book's central symbol and theme: as Iphigenia was sacrificed at Aulis to Artemis, goddess of femininity, fertility and motherhood, so Ellie Hasselmann willingly lays her body upon a sacrificial stone—which she names *Aulis*— giving herself to womanliness and to the mother.

Another myth, Christianity, reinforces for Ellie the idea of self-

*Schmitt's male heroes, by contrast, *can* cope. King David and Rembrandt achieve, they overcome internal and external obstacles, and they become personally fulfilled. No doubt, Schmitt chose them for this reason. And even in some of the books I am discussing here *(The Gates of Aulis, Confessors,* and *The Godforgotten),* where major male figures exist, they can for the most part find resolutions that are impossible for the female.

sacrifice which she carries from this pagan myth. She has both myths in mind; but while her attachment to the Greek one seems imposed upon the matter of the novel rather than inherent to it—seems, in fact, unnecessary and artificial—her connection with Christian myth is fitting. Ellie has inherited the commitment to Christianity from her grandmother, who instilled in her a "theology of pity and fear," and also from a host of ancestors who made a habit of immolating themselves, like bleeding lambs, upon a sacrificial altar. Furthermore, like all the characters—the whole world of the novel—she needs to be connected with an identifying myth of her own time.

The dilemma of her world is described in a lecture by a brilliant, unorthodox Sociology professor, Stephen Maurer. At the core of every culture that ever existed, Maurer says, there was a sustaining myth, a myth "which man has told himself to relieve his despair" (23). And no culture has lasted beyond the day when its myth died. Maurer provides as example the fourth century decline of Rome when the myth of *virtus* was no longer believed. Without *virtus*, roughly defined as manhood and the traits that go with it—honor, strength, and dignity—men in Rome were lethargic, aimless, empty. We, too, Maurer says, live in a time when our cultural myth has decayed. Christianity is passé; without it we can't know what moral values to believe in and live by; we sit idly rotting away, contemplating nothing but death. Maurer prophecies the arrival of the new Socialist myth and announces that modern man must make a choice. He defines, in fact, three available choices: we can identify ourselves with the old, passing legend, embracing the sickness and decay inherent in such an action; we can take on the difficult task of forging an individual legend, like D. H. Lawrence; or we can ride bravely into the future with the new ideology. Stephen Maurer is not a likeable character, and he is ultimately discredited. But his lecture remains a repeated strain in *Aulis,* and his perceptions about cultural myths echo through Schmitt's works. Ellie is the first of the group of Schmitt's women who exist in changing worlds, who must find philosophical underpinnings, and who choose the religious myth, knowing the irony that they can't help doing so.

The action and conflict of the novel arise from Ellie's giving herself to men out of a confused sense of what means will help gain her ends. She thinks that the sacrifice of self for another individual, performed out of pity—as it is sanctioned by religious myth—can make her loved as a woman; she thinks she can resolve her sexuality by giving her body *in place of love.* She thinks so, because this is all she has to give. Deprivation has destroyed Ellie's capacity for loving; she offers pity, loyalty, and gratitude, but she offers nobody love.

In fact, she chooses lovers who evoke pity. Her first lover was a sickly, plainly doomed young man whose death bred in Ellie an excessive and excessively maintained sense of grief and loyalty. She sees in retrospect that sexual intercourse with him was "as it should be. For I did not lie down on a bed; I lay down on an altar, a sacrificial stone. I did not lie down because of desire—how long after that was it that I learned the meaning of the word 'desire'? I lay down for pity, because he had been to his doctor that afternoon, and had come to this room white in the face, and had wanted forgetfulness urgently" (112).

Ellie is equally sensitive about her relationship with her second lover, Eugene McVeagh. Although this relationship, which makes up the central plot of the novel, is more complex, on the whole she doesn't find sexual intercourse with him pleasant and in fact recoils somewhat from his touch. She takes him, too, out of pity, because he's old (in his forties) and dry and needs sexual rejuvenation. Ellie takes McVeagh also because he seems likely to fulfill her needs in other ways. His politeness and gentlemanliness dazzle her; she has never known such courtship. His superiority in age and social class suggest that with him she can act out her romantic wish to subordinate herself to a man. He praises her paintings and buys one for what seems to her a great sum. And through his superficial resemblance to a bust of Julius Caesar, he reminds her of a solid culture, though he's anything but masculine. Most important, she takes him because she imagines he can give her the love her mother failed to give her and the male identity her father failed to give her. The symbolic substitution of McVeagh for both mother and father is beautifully embodied in a scene where McVeagh first holds Ellie in his arms, rocking and cradling her, and then makes love to her. It is their best moment together and their best love-making. Afterwards Ellie says to McVeagh: "You are a magnificent lover; you have so much *virtus*, more than I ever knew could be in a man, and I'm very grateful that you gave it to me" (501).

The inability to love is objectified further in Ellie's brother, Carl, who is in part a double for her. Carl dramatizes another perspective on Ellie's conflicting desires for self-fulfillment and self-abnegation; and he represents also her latent wish for male identity. Like Ellie, he yearns for self-sacrifice, but through social action. Claiming that he wants to serve all humanity, he espouses Maurer's Socialism, the new myth, as his means of serving. But Carl is plainly too narcissistic —absorbed, like Buddha contemplating his own navel, in himself— to give of himself for the masses. He can't even bring himself to touch individuals, least of all the girl who wants him. At bottom, he too can't resolve his sexuality, and in fact he worries a good deal about his possible homosexuality. The intertwining and inter- dependence between Carl and Ellie stand in contrast to the other interpersonal relationships in the novel, which are distinctly distant.

Inevitably, McVeagh at last must recognize the many-layered distance between Ellie and himself, a distance created superficially by the difference between them in social status, but more by his adherence to the worst of myths—Capitalism—and most fundamen- tally by the universal lack of love in this world. Not surprisingly, when he forces this same recognition on Ellie, by leaving her for another, womanly, woman, one of his own social group, she can't face up to it. Ellie's neurotic and constant death wish becomes acute. At a retreat where she has gone with Carl, she dives down among the rocks in a lake—throws her body upon a stone and comes up bleeding. The attempted suicide serves all her needs: in social terms, the sacrifice confirms her commitment to the Christian myth; in psychological terms, it pays for her anger at her parents and for the guilt of not being loved or loving; in emotional terms, it attempts to end the despair over repeated rejection and failure to establish her identity as a woman.

There are, finally, affirmations in *Aulis,* but they merely emphasize the male/female dichotomy. Carl rescues Ellie/Iphigenia. He goes down into the water after her and returns holding her. Having touched the slime from the bottom of the lake on Ellie's skin, he accepts human flesh, which is "nurtured in slime"; for the first time he has felt true pity. Having been disillusioned earlier about Maurer and Socialism, Carl is now quite ready to exchange Socialist idealism for practising Christianity. Not only does he become more balanced and whole, but he can choose to do something to verify this cure. At the end Carl takes up his woman and takes on an unfinished teaching job. But for Ellie, the outcome is somehow less satisfying. By giving herself, she has accomplished the sexual res- urrection of McVeagh and is indirectly responsible for the resurrec- tion of Carl—but both have deserted her. By acting out the mythic role of self-sacrifice, she is released from the bind that inhibited her painting and will probably paint better because she will paint realistically her own world, not her romantic, imagined one. By trying to assuage her excessive desire for self-destruction she, like Carl, can become more whole and better balanced. But we suspect that while she may go about it more sanely in the future, she'll go on giving herself: her sexuality remains essentially unresolved.

The artistic weaknesses of *Aulis* result primarily from Schmitt's failure to integrate so much emotional and intellectual material. The connection between Ellie's feelings and the societal need for a cultural base is somewhat tenuous. Also, even though Ellie's religious commitment, via her ancestors, is convincing, we aren't comfortable with the large dimensions of Greek, Roman and religious myth in such immature characters and in such a mundane world. By contrast, *Alexandra* (Dial Press: New York, 1947), written five years later and after the large historical novel *David the King,* is a short, relatively uncomplex work. This novel, like *Aulis,* is set in what must be Pittsburgh, but the moral dilemmas posed are fully appropriate to the characters and their world. Schmitt's concern with her heroine's sexuality and role crisis remains in the spotlight, is never diminished or blurred by imposed philosophical questions. The focus stays on the heroine's identification through art—specifically, on her accomplishment as an actress, and on the traits and problems that go with such accomplishment.

The character is one of Schmitt's best, a fantastical, unforgettable woman. The key to Alexandra Hill is that she goes to extremity in everything she does. She is always playing a scene, and playing it with just a touch more immersion than is necessary—from the child who lies on the grass in her voile dress crying "O pardon me, thou bleeding piece of earth," to the mature Joan of Arc who is a miracle to the critics. She loves, or to be precise loves her dream of love, extremely; and she carries her loyalty to her men beyond all reason. As a child she acts crazy, "like a monkey," when she is rejected, thereby revealing the extreme sensitivity and vulnerability that cause suicidal despair later, when she is rejected. For all this excessiveness, we understand and accept Alexandra: what saves her is the ironic eye of the narrator, her best friend Sophie. To Sophie, Alexandra is from the beginning "ungodly clever," but "a fool, a poor damned fool."

While Alexandra's excesses are by no means exclusively female, she is yet singularly feminine, as Schmitt's heroines go. Acting is perhaps the only area of accomplishment that can so clearly emphasize feminine charm and beauty. And the plain, skinny Alexandra does become enchantingly beautiful and graceful on stage. Even offstage she learns to dress and groom herself to look, ironically, like "an exquisite and flattering portrait of herself" (233).

And yet, paradoxically, Alexandra can't find herself in this feminine identity. The beauty, Alexandra suggests, is an illusion created by the actress: the star of St. Joan says, "Some people are born beautiful and others make themselves beautiful. The ones who were born beautiful—they walk about as if they were gods, but the others always know. . . . " (251). Furthermore, even when Alexandra has become a star, she continues to need to search for love and to lean dependently on those closest to her. As a child she dreamed that if she were famous everybody would love her, and she could not then be wounded. But the dream can never come true for her, essentially because no matter how many people-at-large love her, they can't protect her from being hurt by the denial of love from a particular, and unavailable, somebody. She can't feel secure as a woman, can't resolve her sexual identity, no matter what she achieves.

Alexandra's sense of unworthiness and unwomanliness comes from primary sources. Like Ellie, she has parents who don't care about her. As a child she tells Sophie, "They haven't the slightest notion of what I really am. Besides, they love each other so much, they have no room left for loving me" (135). Alexandra would surely be loved if she were like her mother, who has "a scent of clean womanliness about her—sudsy bath-water, talcum, and newly washed, sun-dried hair" (30). Another rejection, by the mother of Alexandra's teenage Jewish boyfriend, Emmanuel Saltzman (a promising musician who is crippled by the tie to his mother), reinforces the original devastation: "Any *shicksa* is bad enough, but a *shicksa* like you—a plain, ugly *shicksa* without even a good shape . . . " (87). No wonder Alexandra takes Sophie's warm mother as a substitute, and in this woman's presence remains all her life childlike.

And like Ellie, Alexandra is deprived of a sustaining myth, although the situation here is individual rather than societal as in *Aulis*. The child Alexandra has deep religious faith; she believes that everything will be righted in the hereafter and that all things work as part of God's pattern. It is her own teenage sensitivity and curiosity, and her physical desire for Emmanuel, that bring her to wrestle with doubt and send her to ask questions of the prudish Reverend Kindler. His answers are a scolding, a brush-off by God for her "evil" thoughts. Thus guilt, mixed with defiance and doubt of the kind of God painted by Reverend Kindler, drive Alexandra to lie down on the grass with Emmanuel; and thus the loss of God, and of God's love, become forever a part of her sexuality.

The connection between sexuality and religion is secondary in this novel; it's through art that Alexandra gives herself. Schmitt explores that connection primarily in the interaction between Alexandra and her lover, Kenneth Ellery. This man, the most romantically perceived of Schmitt's lover-figures, was an actor until polio left him with the withered hand and shoulder that ended his pallid career. When Alexandra meets him, he is aging, egotistical, somewhat embittered. But even to the sensible Sophie he represents "the elusive and the unattainable," the essence of experience and taste and tragedy. He enters Alexandra's life in the most romantic way imaginable: she is acting in a high school play, and he appears as a shadowy figure in the balcony, watching her. He brings her flowers on opening night; and then he takes her into his life, becomes her teacher/father/mother—teaches her not only how to act but how to dress, feeds her, nurtures her, *creates* her. And it is, of course, a two way street. Alexandra prostrates herself before him, works herself to exhaustion to please him, and in becoming his actress and his lover, manages to rejuvenate him professionally and sexually.

The paths of Alexandra's love affairs seem inevitable, given their loveless bases. As Emmanuel left, so Ken Ellery leaves. Both, symbolically, fail to appear in the audience as Alexandra triumphs on stage. Her becoming a fine actress doesn't make these "somebodies" love her, because, in fact, they lack the capacity to love. Also, she can't resolve her sexuality through acting because she offers her art in place of love. Alexandra's romantic *idea* of love reveals this pervasive scarcity of real love: she envisions it as "a tremendous harp strung between earth and heaven, swathed in mist, only half-visible to the uninitiate, . . . " waiting to be played upon by two together who will make "rhapsodic music without an end or a beginning, a never-finished music plucked from a never-ending multiplicity of strings" (152).

The truth is that Alexandra's and Ken's intense needs for self-fulfillment eliminate the possibility of their loving each other. Ellery takes Alexandra for her ability to bolster his ego: her pity for his condition, her admiration for his faded elegance, and her gratitude for his help. But he can't sustain the burden of her adoration. And

Alexandra takes him because he supports her art, and because of his capacity to replace father and mother. It is, in fact, because of this latter need that Alexandra can't admit his rejection. She remains senselessly loyal to Ellery, continuing to hope and believe that when she is famous enough he'll want her back, believing it long after she is a star and he is old and tainted, not merely a failed actor but a second-rate agent who trades in cheap comedies.

While the strengths of *Alexandra* lie in these somehow believable excesses, the extremes make resolution difficult. The end of the novel is structurally weak. We're not quite convinced that either Alexandra's need for self-fulfillment in art or her desire for Ken Ellery's return could make her become so ruthless as to ruin others who stand between her and the top of stardom. The act (reported, not dramatized) seems too aggressive or masculine for such a dependent woman, and perhaps too great a perversion of her basic religious principles. Nor can we quite believe that Alexandra's guilt over this ruthlessness causes her to feel so unworthy of being loved that she commits suicide when at last she has a chance for a genuine love relationship with another man, Les Talbot.

Schmitt was, I think, unaware of or unable to bring fully to the surface the motives that can make these events seem psychologically consistent. The act of stepping on others professionally is a metaphor, a disguise for Alexandra's inability to love. When she perceives her non-love finally through a pathetically empty reunion with Ken Ellery in a bar in New York and understands the wasted years of loyalty and romantic longing, she feels guilt for having given all this instead of love. Although the relationship with Les Talbot proves her power to elicit love through art (he fell in love while watching her act St. Joan), she renounces this nurturing, sexual love because she can't return it.

The suicide is structurally sound also in that Alexandra's self-destruction is the acting out of death-wish impulses that have existed from her beginnings. The death wish is expressed in the first scene the child plays for Sophie, a "death" even more convincing than Sophie's own grandfather's death. The suicide evolves from neurosis turned madness, a madness which had been predicted on stage by an adolescent Alexandra playing Ophelia to an off-stage Hamlet who rejected her. In the broadest sense, the death expresses the woman's despair over the impossibility of achieving self-fulfillment through art and fame. Like Ophelia, Alexandra was the more deceived.

Schmitt once said *Alexandra* was the book she needed to get out of her system. Not that such a cathartic motive made it a bad book—indeed, it has a great deal of warmth and immediacy. Alexandra is perceptively made; her vulnerability and her excessiveness are key attributes of the Schmitt heroine. She really is "a poor damned fool," really does need to ask "to be forgiven for asking too much and for offering too much" (314).

Once the question of what art could do for a woman was examined—and appropriately, *Alexandra* came after Schmitt's great success with *David,* when it seemed she was on the road to fame—she was free to return to myth, to the exploration of religious, moral values in connection with woman and woman's role. *Confessors of the Name* (Dial Press: New York, 1952), set in Rome when the empire is decaying and Christianity's star is rising, does that in full measure. It's a deep, earnest, big book: for many modern readers, unfortunately, too long, and finally too philosphical. The problem here isn't like that in *Aulis.* By now Schmitt had learned to write in a prose style suited to her material and to build a narrative structure strong enough to carry her themes and to sustain interest; and the accurate historical background, which as in *David* she evokes with great imaginative power, provides characters and a society that can carry the weight of her philosophical interests.

An important part of the reason why *Confessors* gets little attention now, I suspect, has to do with its un-modern examination of the possibility of heroism by means of religious martyrdom. So many of us don't quite believe in it, finally. And this is a shame, because it's through religious martyrdom, a literal self-sacrifice in the Roman amphitheater, based on the example of Christ and on the principles taught by Paul, that the heroine, Paulina, achieves her unique place among Schmitt's women. Paulina expresses the desire to espouse wholeheartedly, without question, pure Christianity, as she expresses the asexual, spiritual ideal of Christianity. She is Schmitt's most fulfilled, most successful woman. Even though the novel has a male protagonist (Paulina's cousin, Favorinus), Paulina becomes the more important hero.

For all this success, the twenty-nine year old Paulina resembles Schmitt's other heroines in predictable ways. To begin with, although her voice is warm and womanly, and her eyes full of compassion, she is a thin, colorless being whom "nobody would have looked at twice"; and she has "the aspect of a prematurely aging child"

(27, 29). She appears most markedly childlike and dependent in her relationship with her husband, Probus, who (like Eugene McVeagh and Ken Ellery) is something of a father/teacher to her.

Probus—the name is very apt—merits close examination because he is the first of three similar, insufficient males to whom the Schmitt heroine is bound. A leader of the Christians, he is morally upright but stiff and authoritative; he has an "uncomfortable quality" about him. Physically he is marred by "loose-jointedness, an awkward stance, a stoop that made him seem to be discrediting to himself." A sense of "nameless insufficiency" hangs about him, an insufficiency objectified in the absurd task he has set for himself: for years Probus has been writing an epic, in the style and meter of the *Aeneid,* recounting the wanderings of Barnabas. He pours into this task, it seems, whatever emotion there is in him. Generally he is cold, and although wise in religious matters, he states philosophical and practical truths in a voice so testy it creates arguments among the elders. We have some sympathy for him because he knows what he's like; but we suspect that he can't love others either physically or spiritually.

The marriage, as we would expect, is barren. Paulina talks of spiritual love and lectures to her cousin Favorinus about marriage as a gift of the Lord, given so that people may comfort each other in their loneliness and sustain each other in their terror and suffering as they labor side by side. Having accepted childlessness and an unsatisfactory sexual relationship early in their marriage, Probus and Paulina have actually renounced the flesh, have taken a vow of chastity. While Paulina looks restlessly at Favorinus, she remains with Probus as the obedient, submissive child and the faithful wife. She is joined to Probus, she tells Favorinus, because she is a Christian, once and forever, in this world and the next. Paulina and Probus express deep tenderness and concern for each other as they encounter the dangers of this world, but her longing for the next world has suggestive overtones; and clearly their tie arises, as Favorinus notes, out of mutual pity born of mutual fear.

The fear is, in fact, sound. The Rome of the novel is the very world described by Professor Maurer in *Aulis,* where the old, formerly sustaining myth of *virtus* must defend itself against the new myth of Christianity, and does so by means of persecution. But if to choose Christianity is dangerous, the choice gives one tremendously sustaining power of social commitment and action. Paulina's movement into the new era contrasts with the frustrated stagnation of the patrician Favorinus, who sees the decay and impotence of the old myth, yearns for something to hang onto, but hesitates to accept the new values.

Not surprisingly, we can detect personal motives for Paulina's zealous religious commitment. Like Ellie Hasselmann, who in seeking her female identity invests all her hopes in sexual intercourse, equating it with love and therefore asking it to do too much, so Paulina invests everything in religious intercourse. Her malady is no less extreme. Paulina utterly denies sexual desire (except on a single climactic occasion when she submits to the emotion between her and Favorinus and lies down with him). She offers her spiritual energy to the world in the same way Ellie offers her body. But she is on safer ground; she has found a mode of action that sanctions the female "virtues" of chastity and renunciation—that not only sanctions them, but affords positive identification and human dignity through them.

Thus Paulina finally is different from her predecessors in *Aulis* and *Alexandra* primarily in finding a more socially appropriate, therefore successful, outlet for the sexuality crisis. Her commitment to myth/religion, because it takes place in a setting hospitable to such commitment, can become meaningful in a way impossible for Ellie. While Alexandra's drive for self-fulfillment through giving herself as an artist emerges ultimately as selfish, Paulina's self-fulfillment occurs through real service to others, and thereby establishes her worthiness. Her true commitment to social action through the myth reminds us of Carl's pseudo-commitment to Socialism; but whereas Carl was impotent in an unsuccessful cause, Paulina is fertile. She teaches Favorinus about Christianity (note the role reversal here) and brings him into the fold (even though his conversion takes place after her death); she creates a rebirth in him. And she is, therefore, indirectly responsible for the rebirth of faith among some of the imprisoned, disheartened Christians, a rebirth which occurs as a result of the conversion of Favorinus. If Paulina, like the heroines before her, can't give sexual love, she substitutes for it genuine spiritual love; and in exchange, she gets love from her flock. Through this love she achieves a female role and identity as mother and teacher to her adopted children—her novices—and becomes, symbolically, a Holy Mother.

Paulina's relation to Schmitt's other heroines comes out forcefully in her crimson confession—the powerfully drawn moment when she leads a group of Christians, all of whom have freely chosen

116

confession and self-sacrifice, into the Roman Amphitheater to face the lions. Here the split male/female, Carl/Ellie characterization, as well as Ellie's longing for *virtus,* come to fruition. Paulina gets male power. It is she who bolsters the others' failing courage, she who waits to endure the last and hardest death—she who experiences the mythic nobility and heroism of the occasion. And metaphorically, her female sexuality is fulfilled at the moment "when her body [goes] down under the weight of the lion" (426). Giving her self for the sake of God and humanity, Paulina achieves self-discovery.

But not without some irony and ambiguity. After her adultery with Favorinus she renounced his love and then relieved her guilt by giving herself up to the Christian-hunting Romans. Later, in prison, she confessed to one of the elders. The source of her guilt, she said, was not just that she loved Favorinus, but "that I took from him what I never had in Probus, and by holding out my hands to take it I made plain that Probus was insufficient, and I—I who leaned on his steadfastness and knew him and the worth of him better than any of the others—I who was his only companion—I should never have let my restless, seeking heart betray me into showing, even to myself, even before one other man, that my dear yoke-fellow in Jesus was not enough—" (402). While the lion scene is Paulina's most triumphant moment, this confession is her most human moment. Having been able to give Probus only her loyalty, she is broken by her disloyalty. Even the spiritual love she feels equally for the two men at the instant of her death can't entirely wash away the sin of demonstrating her husband's inadequacy by sharing her sexual impulses with another man.

In retrospect we might wonder where Schmitt could have gone next with her heroine, after this relative high, this blossoming of imagined reality. In actuality, she must have had little choice. It was terribly unfortunate for her, but ultimately fortunate for her writing, I think, that her emotional breakdown in 1962 and the accompanying depression sent her back to re-examine the old, unresolved concerns. Out of new suffering, Schmitt brought to her last two novels, *Electra* (Harcourt, Brace and World, Inc.: New York, 1965) and *The Godforgotten,* a deeper insight into her heroines— conscious acknowledgment of their problems and overt yet controlled revelation of their psychic and philosophical dimensions.

Schmitt's selection of the Electra myth as subject matter seems almost fated. She had thought of it first when she was eighteen or twenty. Now, there was the obvious relationship between the psychological implications of the story and what she was meeting in her own psychoanalysis. But to look at the novel, and draw parallels between fiction and life, only in this light is both too easy and unjust. The selection of Electra continued and furthered Schmitt's lifelong interest in the past, in myth as the basis of cultural values and societal stability, and in the power of myth to express essential truths. Furthermore, in Electra's story Schmitt found the opportunity to explore and depict, in the darkest period of her own life, the female unable to resolve her obvious sexual crisis, the female caught among conflicting commitments, the female trapped between awful choices.

In Electra's character and situation we find certain aspects of earlier heroines played out to their logical destination (given the author's present perception of the world), and at the same time imbued with metaphoric and symbolic meaning. Descriptions of Electra's physical appearance, for example, both remind us of Ellie, Alexandra and Paulina and fill in some of the implications of their physical appearances. Here is how an old man of the town sees Electra: "He knew her by her boyish straightness . . . her skin was sallow, her sea-colored eyes were not large enough for real beauty . . . " (7,14). She is hauntingly thin because she has eaten at bare subsistence level since her father, Agamemnon, went off to fight the Trojans. Her mother, Clytemnestra, believes that "The strangeness of [Electra's] beauty—for beauty she had, though it was of a subtle and unusual kind—had led her to see herself as unbeautiful" (61). Electra sees herself also as unfeminine: she hates the court occasions when she has to dress in such a way as to display her womanhood, baring her pointed, insufficient breasts. All these descriptions foreshadow Electras's central male/female identity crisis. On the one hand, when she wants to defy her mother, she does so by appearing in desperately feminine, indeed brazen, outfits—a scarlet robe, gold shoes, and the tallest crown she can find. On the other hand, we're never allowed to forget her identity with her brother, Orestes: they were "like two plums growing from a single divided stem, . . . so like that it was almost impossible to tell them apart, forever intertwined" (11).

Electra's identity problem clearly stems from the family relationships. And here again, the elements of these relationships are familiar to us, but more acute. Although, as Clytemnestra tells

Electra, Agamemnon was bitter that Electra, his first child, was a female, Electra and Orestes always sided with the father against the mother. In his absence during the Trojan War, Electra has made an idol of Agamemnon. And he clearly shows affection for her when he returns from Troy. But he is a harsh, egotistical and impatient man, surely hard to love. Electra's relationship with her mother is even more difficult. Clytemnestra's favorite was always the other daughter, the beautiful and feminine Iphigenia, whom Agamemnon has given to Artemis at Aulis in exchange for good winds to carry him to Troy. Clytemnestra herself is aware that she finds no pleasure in Electra and has never loved her. However, in a confrontation where Clytemnestra asks Electra for sympathy and gets none, we recognize the pain of being unloving and unloved on both sides.

Clytemnestra, like Orestes, represents an aspect of Electra and of the Schmitt heroine. She is the mature woman, preening and painting herself to look young and feminine, seeking almost too late to fulfill a womanly destiny. It's made quite clear that Agamemnon never loved Clytemnestra—that he was cold and hard to her, that he merely used her as sex object and bearer of children. We can understand the need that drives her to Aegisthus, one of the few men left in Mycenae.

Schmitt's Aegisthus has telling insufficiencies. Physical incapacity has kept him from going to war with the other men. He is aging, bald and spindle-shanked, and "his belly was limp in spite of its thinness, his shoulders were narrow and sloped forward" (25). Aegisthus gives Clytemnestra sexual satisfaction she has never before known, and he is witty as well as politically clever. But the great feast he makes for the people, who refuse to come, reminds us of the waste in Probus' epic. And when things go badly, after they have murdered Agamemnon, Aegisthus weakens; bit by bit his unmanliness comes out. He won't stand with Clytemnestra by Agamemnon's corpse; when Clytemnestra becomes ill, Aegisthus is "like a piece of straw"; and at last, filled with terror, he is sexually impotent. Clytemnestra's tie to him, arising out of loneliness, becomes finally loyalty born of mutual guilt, marked partly by thinly stretched tenderness and pity, partly by hate and fear.

The only person with whom Electra has a mutually loving relationship is her brother, Orestes; and this relationship raises many ambiguous questions, not only about identity and possible incestuous desire, but most important, about further loss and deprivation. Like the Carl/Ellie figure in *Aulis,* only in more complex ways,

Electra and Orestes become doubles, male/female aspects of a single personality. Their closeness in childhood and the metaphor of the plum branch are inescapable: they are one. But like Agamemnon, Orestes has gone away; learning of his mother's adultery and realizing the danger of this knowledge, he leaves Electra to take on the responsibility of dealing with Mycenae. Electra has a dream about him, full of significant details: he returns to Mycenae wearing a cloak she has embroidered, and she thinks, "he must love me still"; although he has been to no battle, he drops the cloak and stands in his loincloth to show "his manliness, his honorable wounds, his princely body"; Electra weeps because "his delicate and blameless person was not as it had been"—his arms are those of his father, and his chest is that of the warrior Eurymedon (whom Agamemnon wants Electra to marry); when she sees that Orestes' smile has lost its old innocence and mocks her, Electra says to him, "So you, too, have deceived me. Where was it, my brother, and with whom?" (195-196). On all sides, Electra is faced not just with remoteness, but with literal desertion.

Electra, as we might well expect, turns off from marriage and especially from sex. She shrinks from the would-be husbands chosen by her parents. She is stiff and ungracious with Eurymedon, feeling sure he couldn't possibly want her. The knowledge of her mother's adultery makes sex hideous to Electra. She is more than coldly innocent about it. Her imagination of the sexual act between Clytemnestra and Aegisthus is a marvel of concreteness and fascinated disgust. "Flanks, buttocks, the smells of excretion . . . Secret hair and slippery wetness and the member swollen and purplish and arrogant . . . Those two, stuck together, become one beast by joining their bestial parts . . . It seemed to her then that they, in their loathsome transport, were at the core of the world, that the world was rocked by their thrustings and strivings, made putrid with their exudations, made rotten enough to fall apart" (57).

While we're caught up in the emotional reality of these characters, we're equally aware of the mythic dimensions of the world of this novel. The culture of Mycenae rests on an ancient myth, basically a religious one, which establishes its moral values. The people remain loyal to Agamemnon because he fulfills the requirements of the myth. Although he has been harsh and indifferent to their needs, he is a just king. We know that the code of ethics is itself without compassion, harsh but just: it implacably demands that the ruling House of Atreus pay out retribution for the sins of its ancestors. In the present time of the novel, however, a surface uneasiness of moral values exists, caused by the absence of Agamemnon. A new "myth" or set of values is represented in Aegisthus, or the Aegisthus-Clytemnestra team. The adulterous, unsanctioned relationship marks a sinking into moral degradation—not simply because the Queen goes sneaking into a lover's bed at night, but more because the man who now wields power in Mycenae isn't bound by the old code, and is devious and shifty.

It seems to Electra that it is her personal burden to decide which side will win when Agamemnon returns. Schmitt shows us how terrible, how impossible, her choice is. If she doesn't tell Agamemnon of Clytemnestra's unfaithfulness—and quickly—Clytemnestra and Aegisthus will murder him. If she tells Agamemnon, he will kill Clytemnestra (and Aegisthus). Her loyalties lie most with Agamemnon, both because of her childhood love for him and because of her commitment to the old moral code and to the people of Mycenae—and somehow, too, because his unfaithfulness with Cassandra bothers her less than Clytemnestra's adultery. But in a nightmare Clytemnestra appears headless and bloodied, bringing home Electra's unavoidable guilt. Not only does she bear the mythic guilt of the House of Atreus, but also, since both parents have rejected her, she is bound either way to feel double guilt, once for having brought about the destruction of a human being and an order, and once for having wished it.

Electra is actually powerless—and partly because she is a woman. As she could not, like Orestes, have fled and made her way alone through the mountains, so now she cannot solve anything with a sword. Her gods, the compassionless representatives of the old myth, appear in her dreams as a procession of ancestors, urging her to carry out her sworn resolution to tell Agamemnon. But Agamemnon, in the way of Greek drama, participates in his own doom. Electra goes to tell him, but he won't listen; he is absorbed with his hopes for marrying Electra to Eurymedon in order to make Eurymedon his successor. This denial of Orestes, which is essentially a denial of herself, is too much for Electra. Denouncing, or renouncing, Agamemnon's false and fickle heart, she feels that the last vestige of her childish love for him is gone. The subsequent murder of her father, however, drives her to self-sacrifice and madness.

It is self-sacrifice, or a giving up of the self, on several levels, literal and metaphoric. With Aegisthus' men after her, she flees from the palace to the common people in the town, hides among them and becomes one of them. Then, in exchange for her identity as princess she takes on the role of social savior: a lion stalks the fields near the town, and only Electra can safely go out to gather the roots and sticks that prevent starvation. Soon she begins to hallucinate and changes her identity further. Exhausted and terrified, she becomes the lion, capable of carrying out the punishment for which she feels responsible. She imagines herself, in the lion's body, visiting Clytemnestra and Aegisthus in their bed, or reporting to Agamemnon in his tomb. At other times, she doubts whether she is woman or man, since she now looks exactly like Orestes: "Her hair was cropped and she wore a boy's straight brown tunic cut off above the knees; and, since her breasts had grown sore with all the reaching and bending, she had bound them down flat with linen bands. So, seeing her image in water or at the bottom of a copper cauldron, she would think how, if her brother ever returned, nobody would be able to tell the two of them apart. 'I am not his sister,' she would say to herself, wrenching at the dead branches. 'We were born twins, both boys, and our hands were clasped in the womb, and we came forth hand in hand' " (272). She waits for Orestes to come, so that together they can discharge their duty to revenge the murder of Agamemnon—that is, to kill Clytemnestra. But Orestes doesn't come, and because Electra brings danger to those who harbor her, she must leave the town. She goes, with a knife, intending actually to sacrifice herself: "If I myself do it in the hillside above the tombs, my father's bones will know of it, and he will accept me as a sacrifice and forgive me what the gods and the ancestors cannot forgive" (300).

Orestes comes upon her in the field and prevents the death. The reader is left to imagine the working out of their destiny; the book is aborted, unfinished. And the ending is too easy and not quite convincing. But what we have, when looked at in the light of the progression of Schmitt's heroine, is important. Electra's morbid obsession with Clytemnestra's sexual life, and her own clearly delineated inability to accept herself as a female, let alone as sexual object, spotlight inescapably the major source of her identity crisis. Electra's fantasied resolution through metamorphosis—the taking on of a lion-self, which represents not only male-ness, power and authority, but also symbolic identity with the House of Atreus and its myth (remember the great Lion Gate at the entrance to Mycenae) —points out in one forceful image the futility of the heroine's desire to resolve the sexuality crisis through fidelity to a myth. And finally, Electra's madness—for her breaks from reality and her near-suicide are nothing less—reveals the despair that must accompany awareness of such a dilemma and of one's aloneness in the face of it.

The Godforgotten (Harcourt Brace Jovanovich, Inc.: New York, 1972) contains all of these elements, in some sense, but it deals with them in a more richly ambiguous way. The heroine achieves at the same time resolution and frustration, acceptance and despair. Partly this new dimension in the woman may be due to the presence of a male protagonist who takes on, and resolves, some of the same sexual and spiritual dilemmas she does, and thereby helps her move toward resolution. But also, the added dimension is surely due to the author's enhanced understanding and slightly new stance. Schmitt here seems sure of what she knows about her heroine; and she faces up to the limitations of her heroine's life. Furthermore, in this novel Schmitt synthesizes, better than ever before, knowledge of her character and theme with knowledge of her craft. The prose is spare and eminently appropriate; the events are what *would* happen, given these characters in this world. The psychological materials given raw exposure in *Electra* have now been transformed by the imagination; thought and feeling are revealed, and multiplied, through metaphor and symbol. *The Godforgotten* is Schmitt's finest book—even, I believe, one of the finest books of our time.

Because of this tight integration of the elements of the story, we can't talk about Julianne, the heroine, except in relation to all other elements. The need for identity and moral values is focused first in the world of the novel. As for the characters, the sexual and moral dilemmas are focused centrally in the protagonist, Father Albrecht. The heroine here takes a secondary place—woman's place.

The need for myth is the essential nature of the society Schmitt has created in *The Godforgotten;* and as the imagined embodiment of the mythless society, the world becomes itself mythic. Further-more, this world with no myth for people to believe in, no clear moral foundation for people to stand upon, is like our own society, viewed Existentially—especially since the novel is concerned with the consuming question of the loss of Christianity and the moral values it teaches. We are in the stronghold of Christian faith and dogma, medieval Europe—but only tangentially and for purposes of ironic contrast. Actually, the world of the novel exists outside Europe, outside the Church, even, metaphorically, floating outside time and space. It is an island just off the mainland, formerly a monastic community connected to the rest of the world by an isthmus, but now cut off by an earthquake and tidal wave which submerged the land bridge. Because the earthquake occurred around the year 1000 A.D., the survivors on the island assumed they were so unworthy that they had been overlooked by God at the apocalypse. Their descendants have struggled on in despair for a hundred years, believing themselves the only people left in an empty, meaningless world. Although the isthmus has reappeared, they think there's nothing to be found in the space on the other side. Not only are they isolated and alienated from man and God, but they have lost the sense of time; they number years from the "termination" of the world. And they have forgotten almost completely the order, the ritual, and the values of the Church. The overt symbol of their loss exists in an inland lake formed at the time of the tidal wave: the old cathedral, submerged in the lake, mystically beckons them, while the waters give off an awful stench and threaten to bring up again such foetid relics as the wafer that poisoned one of the early abbots.

In the island of St. Cyprian, we have come full circle to the lifeless culture posited by Stephen Maurer in *Aulis*. We're back with Maurer's question: "How does man get on with complete license—no pattern to follow, no formula to repeat, no gods to jog his elbow when he steps outside the given line? . . . How does man get on, legendless man, walking where he will among the shattered pieces of a broken civilization?" (245). We're back with his answer, too: in the dark, rotten, barren land, "Man sits in lethargy with his hands empty and open," (246) waiting only for death.

Most of the people of St. Cyprian's island fit this description. Their history since the termination is filled with denial of responsibility, self-pity, and despair. But a few of the inhabitants have done just a little better than Maurer predicted. One member of the community, an intelligent and cynical monk named Giraldus, has at least tried to forge his own myth. He rejects completely whatever limp vestige of the old Christian myth remains, on the grounds that if there were a God and a natural order, there should not be such suffering as he sees. To this Existential denial Giraldus adds "intercourse with devils": he has crossed the isthmus many times to take ergot, a prime source of LSD, from the blighted rye growing there. Giraldus has created his own private drug culture; but it serves as a temporary relief, not a cure, and the only one who follows him is a crazy woman. Other leaders of the community have learned to get along, painfully, by the most meager laws of human fellowship. In place of structure and order there exist the simplest rules and punishments by which one's conscience can be relieved. And, lacking given moral values, some have substituted a measure of pity and charity—notably Jehanne, the prostitute who gives her body to those in need; and Julianne, wife of the lord Alain, who takes care of people.

The unbearable emptiness of life on St. Cyprian shows up especially in the relationship between Julianne and her lord Alain. Like former Schmitt heroines, only now twenty years married, the woman is tied to a cold, unloving man. Early on in her marriage she had learned "what it was to be possessed and yet passed through" as though she were a shadow (118). Now Alain is always remote and abstracted; his "quicksilver eyes" evade Julianne's efforts at contact. In bed or out of it she can only wait, and hope that he will notice her—which is unlikely, since all his attention is centered on, his mind obsessed with, his project: he is trying to construct a replica of the sunken cathedral out of small, colored stones he finds on the beach. Julianne's bearing in relation to Alain, and to his project as well, is totally submissive. Having virtually nothing else to do with her time, she is grateful for every crumb of his attention, for each small kindness she gets from him.

Beneath Julianne's surface submission to the marital situation lie suppressed feminine needs. At times anger and sexual desire well up in her. She enjoys flirting with the renegade monk, Giraldus. She regrets that she is losing with age whatever womanly beauty she once had. Her childlessness is another source of anguish. Her insufficiency on all scores drives her to take on substitute children in the community, but mostly to talk herself into a state of dreary resignation.

Into this situation, then, comes the monk Albrecht, sent by the Pope to restore the community to the Church—to bring to it the new/old myth. Albrecht seems physically and spiritually unfit to bear such a heavy mantle. He, too, at almost fifty, is aging. More important, he lacks essential faith in the myth. Disillusioned many years earlier by the corruption he saw in the Church, and soured by his own forbidden and repressed sexuality, he has retreated into self-centered intellectual pursuits and an inherent snobbery. His heart is half-dead. But his journey to St. Cyprian's has begun to prepare him for his task; it's a mythic journey, full of adventures and trials. He loses his way in a dark forest, an underworld; he finds a new town, a visionary or ideal place; and finally, near starvation, he eats the blighted rye containing ergot, hallucinates wildly, and almost dies. His fellow monk carries him to Alain's castle, where Julianne takes care of him. He is as helpless as a baby; she brings about a rebirth.

Father Albrecht's imposed churchly order, and the choice he presents to the St. Cyprians, create as many hardships as they cure. True, he does set time going by establishing division of the day into patterns of ritual, he does put people to work restoring the nunnery and the chapel, and he does move the St. Cyprians back into touch with the world. But the God he delivers is harsh, accusing them of blasphemy and sloth, lust and fornication, and promising death by fire to non-believers. Albrecht gives the St. Cyprians one year to choose between this myth and a frightening freedom: either they stay on the island and join the restored monastic order, or they go out into an unknown world. Most of the islanders choose finally to stay, partly in loyalty to their families; but their personal relationships and their simple values have been disrupted, while the best they can give the myth is approval of the ritual that regulates time, and lingering doubt about the truth of the legend of Christ become man.

It is in the area of self-discovery that Albrecht serves best during that year. The love between Albrecht and Julianne and their sexual and personal fulfillment through each other—their submission to ripeness—release and restore him. Ironically, it takes the public exposure of their affair and of his hypocrisy to reveal to him his own fraudulence. Together, the love and the exposure lead him to self-recognition and to understanding and appreciation of the Cyprian, human values of pity and charity which he had not before perceived. Through Julianne, Albrecht gets a living heart, a true rebirth. Though Julianne chooses in the end to stay on St. Cyprian's and he must leave the island without her, he has gone through enough, and he dies fulfilled in the new town. And by an ironic twist, Julianne's betrayal of her husband causes Alain too to face up to the fraudulence and waste of his life, and even, at last, to feel pity for her. When he destroys his childish cathedral of stones and takes on the responsibility of governing the new order as Abbot of St. Cyprian's, we recognize the possibility that his life can take on meaning.

Not so, the woman. For Julianne, the choice is awful, the resolution darker, the affirmation far more equivocal. But there *is* affirmation. The love and sexual fulfillment that blossom, brief though they are, represent a kind of victory that Schmitt had never before described for a woman. In bed with Albrecht, Julianne is fully woman. It is as if Schmitt were released somehow, after *Electra,* after the breakdown and psychoanalysis, from whatever caused her inability to portray female sexual fulfillment. On top of this femininity, we have affirmation of Julianne's female identity as the mother, a role pointed to throughout the novel. When Albrecht regained consciousness after his illness in the forest, he found the giving hands that tended him eloquent with compassion, and thought that Julianne resembled the church statues of the Virgin Mary. Fittingly, Julianne chooses at the end to become Abbess of the nunnery, a mother superior. And this, too, is a new role for Schmitt's heroine; only Paulina approached it, and she died in it rather than lived in it. Furthermore, by choosing to stay on the island, Julianne asserts her own values, human values of loyalty and compassion and responsibility. And Julianne's standing by her commitment to Alain and to the future generations of St. Cyprians, for whom she will serve as an example of guilt and penitance, becomes a self-sacrifice through which she discovers her self. She tells Albrecht truly: "Were I to go now from my husband, . . . then I would be otherwise than I was when I tended you . . . and lay with you" (299).

But at what price? What does she really have, and what has she given up? Obviously, she has given up sex, she has given up the feel of the flesh she and Albrecht discovered. She has renounced her love, though it was a good and true love. And she has given up the world, the new town which offers resurrection and life. In these senses, her choice is a metaphor for death-in-life—a kind of suicide. Yet the tragedy of Julianne lies most fully in her sane perception of what is left to her. She has a memory: "What we have had of each other was a ripeness . . . We have been fortunate in that we harvested in the ultimate hour" (229). Julianne claims that ripeness is all; but in so claiming, she acknowledges the evanescence of the woman's sexual fulfillment. She has, also, a myth, a new/old myth, which she half believes: she tells Albrecht, "Though I go as God's bride—for so they speak of it—I am no man's bride but yours, no, not even God's" (299). But in so going, she has exchanged one submissive role for another. And she has done so lacking the conviction, let alone the fervor, with which Paulina gave herself to God. Julianne has, finally, one more thing—her terrible realism. When Alain tells her of his hope for a new life in the monastery, she thinks "how men, in spite of their vaunted hard-headedness, believe in a resurrection in this life, and fix their dreams of it upon a certain place," be it a cell in a monastery or a new town. She tells her husband to go and not to worry about her, for "I am a woman, too grounded in the past to renounce it for another life" (298). Unlike Schmitt's other heroines, Julianne is willing to stay on after renunciation. She can settle for less, though she is not less able.

Her resignation points up the bitter acceptance, the ironic affirmations with which Schmitt came at last to view woman's lot and woman's dilemma. The heroine—that one woman in all five women—knows that she can't be a mythic hero or a star, any more than she can be a beautiful, sexual woman; she *cannot* resolve her sexuality in these ways. The best she can do is to take whatever female role is left to her, whatever joy she can find, within the context of her chosen myth. When Julianne lays her body upon the stones of the ancient nunnery, she makes the sacrifice knowing what she stands to gain, little as it may be. Her final stance echoes Schmitt's own longing, expressed at the end of *Sonnets for an Analyst,* to return to the comfort and dignity of religious faith—to believe the old, passing legend, whether or not it still exists: "If God is dead, then show me to his grave," she says. The last of Schmitt's heroines reveals the urge to cling to whatever shred of stability we have known. That's not very much for a woman to have come to, after all.

Equivocal as is the vision in these novels, so is the relationship between the writer and her characters. It's true that through the five heroines Schmitt reiterated personal concerns and explored possible answers. It's true that much of what these heroines are reflects her personal limitations and the limitations her world put on her. But at the same time, we must perceive the work of the creative imagination. As Schmitt said in a lecture (April 17, 1968, Carnegie-Mellon University), "Art is a projection of the artist, what he wishes he could be, but in his life, cannot be." Her point was that the human being who creates characters is insufficient by comparison with them: "*They* are noble—we are base. *They* glitter—we are shadows." If there is some of her abiding sense of personal unworthiness in this thought, there is also a sense of belief and pride in what art can accomplish. Schmitt expressed this perception of the ironic relationship between the artist and art in one of her best sonnets (#47).

> How many noble selves did Shakespeare fling
> To death against the gimcrack scenery
> So that his emptied husk might hold to see
> The green of Stratford through another spring.
> How many Christs were flogged and nailed and hung—
> In oil on wood or canvas—so that Bosch
> Could draw his draught of yellow beer and slosh
> The fiery ghost of life around his tongue.
> Oh, we are fools to send such deputies
> Ahead of us to death. Could we devise
> A shabbier joke than to materialize
> In our hunched greyness after such as these?
> Brave Tristan died—he could have done no less—
> And shoddy Wagner lived to dwindle on success.

Spring Semester, 1972

Part I
A Memory

Barbara Beyer

Gladys said once that if she ever achieved reincarnation, she'd come back as an owl because she had a sensitive neck and all those feathers would be dreadfully uncomfortable. In a sense, the likeness wasn't far off. She had a voice deeper than an owl's throaty whoooo and plumage richer than his drab featherings. She usually decked herself in sleek pant suits of rust and cream. But I'd say she had more wisdom than that traditionally ascribed to the owl. She had not only knowledge of writing and literature, but most of all a good keen knowledge of people.

The course I took under Gladys—we all called her Gladys, freshman and dean alike—was one of the few graduate classes she ever taught. It was a course in fiction writing, a workshop. We were a seedy lot, coming in afternoons from our work, our own teaching, hunching over the rectangle of tables, concentrating on our cigarettes and coffee in the smudged and dreary classroom. But Gladys had all the energy we needed. As she came through the door, we each sat straighter. Gladys had no time for sloth in her students. She said she could write with someone sitting on her writing table, type with a man perched on the typewriter carriage.

The first day of class Gladys briefly outlined our course. We would follow the same format as the undergraduates. Beginners were beginners. We'd keep a journal, work our way through a series of character exercises. Character, she said, was the base strength of all good fiction. People like to read about people. She quoted a fan

Dr. Barbara Langham Beyer has authored a series of articles on the craft of writing in Youth Magazine. She is currently writing poetry and working on her second book of short stories, one of which has appeared in North American Review. She teaches creative writing at Bethel Park Senior High School in Pittsburgh.

letter she had received after publication of *Rembrandt*. "I am an old woman who scrubs floors with my grandbaby beside me, but I read your book. I cry for you. I cry for me. I cry for my baby grand-daughter." That is what a book must do, she said. We would end the course with an encounter, putting our character in contact with one other character. She gave us the assignments one at a time, winding us ever further into that other being we struggled to develop on the page.

She began by asking us to list ten people we knew whom we found interesting enough to write about for two months. She gave cautions: no one we idolized, for earth supports no angels, and all characters, like all people, are mixtures of good and bad; no one under twelve, for children's problems seldom hold adult readers. Narrow the list to three and then to one. She assured us that the creation on our page would never be the model we held in our minds, for we only know others through our own distorted percep-tions. Still, the fleshed body would plant our one foot firmly in reality while we twirled in creative flights. And so they began. Give your character a body, paint as in a photograph, a frozen moment. Your character wakes up in the middle of the night. He is worried. He goes to the kitchen to eat. What is he worried about? What does he eat? How does he eat? Eating traits reveal much about us. So does stripping. Your character is taking a bath. He has been some-where; he is going somewhere. Write a two page scene with your character as an I narrator. Your character has recurring thoughts. He cannot free his mind. Your character overhears something. He feels guilty with the unwanted knowledge. How does he get rid of the guilt? Write your character's dream. We wound inward and inward until we entered the soul of our creation.

Classes followed a pattern. They were two hours. For one hour we would read aloud our exercises from the previous week, and Gladys would elicit favorable comments from the class. Then, she'd begin on the problems, the weak spots, probing. Why this? Why does he do that? How does he feel here? But she always pulled around to a positive perception again. She was demanding, but nothing we wrote, no matter how hackneyed, was all bad. We always had a core left to build upon. Nourished by the positive, we volunteered for these reading-discussion periods. Our characters grew and developed from exercise to exercise, and Gladys remem-bered their activities, their quirks, from week to week, insisting we become acquainted with the characters developed around the table as with old friends. She'd hold up Raskolnikov as a character more vivid, more a part of her memory than many of her own acquaintances. It was a Raskolnikov and nothing less we were creating. She always quoted the best. Dostoevsky, Tolstoy, Turgenev. The Russians rolled off her tongue in casual acquaintance. Shakespeare, too. And Thomas Mann. She held the German dear.

The second hour she gave our next writing assignment and pulled out her stitchery. As we wrote, she stitched. She was embroidering wild flowers that spring. She was good, designed her own patterns; I believe the stitchery pleased her almost as much as good reviews on her books. While stitching, she made comments from time to time, gave help and encouragement, but mostly she had us writing there under the momentum of her presence. By the end of class, we had the kernels tightly woven into ourselves and could continue on our own. In an hour's drive home, I'd be jotting notes at red lights.

Gladys had an uncanny ability to establish a strong personal bond with each of the twenty of us in the room, as she did with almost everyone who studied under her or worked with her. To each of us she was our own special teacher. She drew us out of ourselves until we dropped our layers of self-protective airs and put honesty on the page.

"Paula has a way with dialogue," she'd say. "She should try a play." "Jim, you did that just right. It would have taken a Tolstoy to do it better, and he'd have needed ten pages." "Isn't Tony's character fascinating? Don't you get a feel of that young priest stumbling at midnight around the parish house kitchen setting up mass for himself?" "Lloyd, incest has such danger of melodrama, but you skirt it nicely." "Loosen up, Diane. How would your grandfather really say that? When you write it like he'd really say it, you'll have a fine piece." Always she coaxed us nearer to our craft.

But the intensity of her teaching was draining her. Already that spring she was not well. She had trouble with her eyes and could not read except through a purple plastic filter, and she took heavy doses of medication. At class break she fled into her office for water, a tranquilizer, a moment of privacy, but she always returned with her usual vigor. It was not until the end of the course that I discovered her energy was not infinite.

She had liked my final paper. Liked it enough to stop me after class to ask me if I would be interested in writing a creative piece as my dissertation, perhaps a book of short stories. "Do you think you have a whole book of stories in you?" she asked. "You know, sometimes people write one story and that's all they have to say." I said I'd like to try to write more. "Good," she said, "I think you have more in you, but you must think so too. I'll schedule you for the year following my sabbatical. You'll have your course work finished, and I'll be through with the dissertation students I'm working with now." She was tired, she said. Her new book, *The Godforgotten,* was finished. Publication had been taxing. She was closing herself up with her family, Si and her daughter and grandchildren, whose arrival she expected the following week. I should contact her after July 28th. She'd be ready to go again by then.

She wrote once in June saying that while taking a good long soak in the bathtub she had reread my story and was surer than ever that it was good, that she wanted to advise me when I was ready to begin my dissertation. "Si liked it, too," she wrote. "His judgment is very good."

In the fall semester, her weakening began to show in class. She encountered Milton, a University of Pittsburgh freshman who had somehow weaseled his way into a CMU upper level class through the university cross-registration system. Milton was a prolific writer, filling page after page, week after week, revising not one word. He was always the first to volunteer to read, but each week's writing was no better than the last. " 'Pass the catsup,' Aunt Rose said pedantically," he read one day.

Gladys protested, "Pedantic means teaching. How can you pass the catsup pedantically?"

"It's an attitude I'm trying to capture," Milton said, his eyes shifting around the table.

"Then show your character teaching. Add it to her dialogue. The word, pedantically, does not show teaching."

His eyes shifted again. "It's probably not worth revising. I have another idea I'm working on now."

"But the aunt is good. If you don't revise, your writing will never get better. My God, do you want it to always be sloppy?"

"This is a good idea I'm writing for next week," he said.

By class break she was shaking. She clutched my arm and said, "My God, let me out of here. I don't think a tranquilizer will do it." But she never gave up on him, never ignored his needs even when he ignored them himself.

Once she took me into her office while she rested, head in hand, sitting in her easy chair. "Are you sure you want to do it?" she asked. "Are you sure you want to study with such an old woman?"

I stared at her. She was a legend across the campus, across the city. Students came to CMU just for the opportunity to study under Gladys Schmitt. "Yes, I'm sure," I said; and she squeezed my arm. That was September. In October she was dead.

But it is through that spring semester that I like to remember Gladys. Hell and damnation, throaty laughter, stitching her wild flowers and threading into us the craft, the discipline, the devotion of her art. I missed the last class meeting because of illness, but to miss was such a disappointment that a friend taped the session for me. Our final papers were in, and class was an open discussion where Gladys freely held forth, urging craft. . . .

Part II
In Class

GLADYS: What was the worst problem you encountered in writing your encounter, and has anybody got suggestions as to how that can be taken care of?

TONY: Mine was deciding what to put in and what to leave out.

GLADYS: I suppose that once you didn't ask yourself that question, you'd go crazy. I remember on one occasion I was working on a vast book which was far too vast and that I wish I had abandoned instead of finishing. It was Confessors of the Name. It was definitely a publication success, but I had a terrible time with it. At the time, a young teacher here who was working in my department under my option said to me one day, "I can very well understand how a person could decide what he wanted to put into the book, but I'll be damned if I can understand how he would decide what he would leave out of it." And suddenly this struck me. I mean it's like saying to a person who is walking on a tightrope, "There's emptiness on either side." I couldn't write for about three weeks after that, forming the notion of how do I know what to leave out.

I suppose you know it intuitively. Once you start, if you feel you're repeating yourself or you're doing something unnecessary, or the scene you have outlined to put in there doesn't seem to be going well, or it doesn't seem to have any light in it, then there would be two questions that you could ask yourself. One would be: Am I doing this from the right point of view or the right angle, have I read the right point of view in the person, and have I started at the right time in it; and the other would be: Do I need this blasted scene at all? Almost every scene that I've planned to do and then eliminated has either been a scene that I didn't need—that I thought I should put in though I could see beforehand that I'd taken care of every dynamic thing that was happening in that scene—or I had chosen a wrong point of view, or I had started the scene too early, or I was kind of creeping up on it slowly instead of leaping right in and doing the action. If you find yourself repetitive and the scene is not going well, then ask yourself, could I leave it out? Otherwise I don't know. I don't know how you know what to put in.

I think also there's always something artificial about what we're doing here. It isn't like really writing a story. Then, you can produce when you please. If you want to let it lie around for a while and then come back to it, chop it, change it, that's all right. The classroom situation—and you ought to realize this too about your students—is always slightly artificial. You have to say there's a certain day everybody must get his blasted papers in. Everybody. Usually three or four people don't, but if you didn't say that, you might get your papers in the middle of August. Everything that you people handed in, if you could now let it lie around for, say two weeks, and then go back and start over again, you'd see a million possibilities that you hadn't seen before. One of the things that would happen, especially if you had an obligation to hand in another version of it, would be that in your preconscious mind all sorts of things would happen about it. You wouldn't think that you were actually thinking about it, but a whole lot of rich unavailable things would begin coming to the surface. This invariably happens after you've got the skeleton of a thing in good order. Then you put flesh on it and it fleshes itself out more and more and more.

Connected with that is the other problem: when the hell do you know when to stop. Because of course if you do a short story and then two weeks later you do another version and two weeks later still another version, it stands to reason that each version will be still better. The only thing is that when you start to do it a fourth or a fifth time, two things happen. Either you are finicky and fussy and bogged down in unnecessary detail or you are what you should be— so damned sick of the thing you hope you never see it again. I would say that three versions with time between are enough for almost anything you want to work on. Some more questions.

DIANE: I thought maybe it was the ten page space limitation that caused this problem. I gave the character very strong emotions and I don't know how quickly they fluctuate.

GLADYS: We had this same problem come up before in Fiction Four where the people are required to hand in twenty pages of consecutive material, fully developed, gone over three times in one semester. One of the girls said, "It's too little. There just isn't enough. Twenty pages is not long enough, and I don't see why we shouldn't hand in twenty pages at mid-term and then twenty more pages at a different time at the end of the semester." One of the boys, who wrote the best story I've gotten in that class, a really stunning story, looked at her and said, "You what? I couldn't take this class."

Then there's a question of how much can you possibly read, and read with attention, and write critical letters on between the time when the papers come in and the time when the grades must be there. You take seventeen and multiply it by twenty, how many pages have you got? And if you take another seventeen and multiply that one by fifteen and add the two together, it's going to end that you have too many pages, and you're really not giving too much sensible attention to anything, no matter how good your eyes happen to be. What do you people do about masses of things coming in at the end of the year?

JIM: Cry.

GLADYS: (Laughter) You cry. I cry a little, too. My husband has always taken my end of the semester agony as being sort of ridiculous on my part. You know, there's the fussing to get over, the terrible, terrible crisis in her academic life—until he started to read them aloud. He feels quite differently about it now. (Laughter)

JOHN: I'm dealing with a very dramatic, almost melodramatic, situation, and there is a very thin hairline between the two. How do I flatten the action out some?

GLADYS: There's one way to test yourself. That is the horrible, embarrassing experience of reading it aloud to yourself in a really dramatic voice. If there's anything wrong with it, it will come out unless you're so hopelessly narcissistic you couldn't deal in empathetic art at all.

By the way, Jim, you were dealing with a situation that was almost unbelievable, and I thought and my husband thought, too, that your keeping to the details and simply rendering the concrete details were the salvation of that whole situation, that if it were going to be done truly—you know, level under level under level— it would take a Tolstoy to do it, and if Tolstoy were doing it, it would take him about ten pages of buildup before he even would get there. But that story had terrifically intense tragic content, and there wasn't one bit of phoniness about it. It was very well planned. Very well planned.

TED: Writing over a fairly long period of time, I found it difficult to get away from the influence of things currently happening. I'd start some place, and then I'd read something, and it would really affect me. I'd have a difficult time getting out of that frame of reference into my own story.

GLADYS: I know that feeling very well. In fact, that's one of the reasons why I always advise people who are beginning to write to tackle short stories or a journal or a novella and never, never a novel, because one changes tremendously, especially at a young age and especially when you are first starting to write. You, yourself, change. Your whole view on life changes. I started three novels when I was in college, and I threw them all away for that very reason. Other influences would come in. You'd read other books, and you'd be off to a different tone in your writing, and then the parts would fall apart. You'd go back and try to put them together, and then the first part didn't seem as authentic as the second, and then it was all mixed up. It was a mess, and finally you threw it out the window. I think when you are in the apprentice stage, it's probably a darn good thing not to commit yourself to a novel unless the subject of the novel is something that is part of your experience, that haunts you terribly, that you just can't imagine giving up.

LLOYD: I had a problem trying to decide whether to do that potentially melodramatic incident of the father trying to rape the daughter. I decided to distance that whole thing by withdrawing from dialogue and having the point of view of the girl with the suggestion of dialogue. The only word of dialogue that was used was one word—Daddy.

GLADYS: Distancing is a great part of it. That's a way to save yourself from melodrama, to withdraw. Another way would be to assume some other person's point of view looking in on it. For instance—it's unthinkable, I wouldn't suggest you do it, John—but supposing you had done that encounter between the two young men and had somebody listen through a window or a door, and then totally skipped the actual account of the self-castration and instead had gotten signs of it through the mind of some rather stupid woman who was at that moment doing something else like looking for nutmeg on the shelf. You can distance yourself; you can pull yourself far, far away, and that will save your skin.

Then there is another device that sometimes works and that is for the narrator, who has the right, who has been inside the person, who has been the working point of view all along the way, at the very end to withdraw, to become almost a historian reporting the end of the event. The place that I know where that is best done is in Turgenev's *Fathers and Sons,* where you get the whole thing in a very, very close stance to it, and then suddenly a withdrawal, and the author says, well, what happened to them all? This happened to that one, and that happened to the other one. As for the young man who was the hero of the thing—you know, he died, and his parents kept going every Sabbath and standing around his grave. That came off because if there was one thing in the world the young man couldn't have stood, revolutionary as he was, anti-religious as he was, not believing in the worth of the body after the mind had departed out of it as he was—nothing would have provoked him more than for his mother and father, who got on his nerves pretty much anyhow, to be standing around beside his grave. Nevertheless, the mother and father have been so convincing throughout with their simple-minded peasant views that you kind of see that he, Turgenev, was the very man who saw the view of the mother and father. You pull way away, and you know that is the end, and you can stop there.

JAN: I wanted to ask about journals. I found better writing in student journals. Much more imaginative.

GLADYS: I wouldn't be a bit surprised. You see, one of the things is, young writers have a notion that there is something that they ought to do that is called writing, and I wish I could explain it. I can't quite get it through. You get short stories from kids that sound as if the kids have taken and made a mash of all the worst elements of the short story that ever existed in any short story on land and sea, and out of this they have made a kind of an ideal of a rotten short story that they personally were obliged to write, and then they have sat down and written it. People want to be writers instead of to write, and they want to write "a short story" instead of something that they want to write. In the journal, the element of it is an extension of myself, it's my affair, it's my business, it's what's going on in me, and furthermore, it doesn't have to follow any form. It doesn't have to be rotten because it doesn't have to be a short story. It doesn't have to be soupy or flowery or flourishing because it doesn't have to be a poem. You understand what I mean? They push form away, and they start to develop material. I've always found journals absolutely terrific. If a kid keeps writing in a note-book for a long, long period with no notion except that he's writing things as he wants to remember them, he will, without knowing what he's doing, develop a style. After he comes out at the other end of that notebook, the only way you can undo his style is to tell him to go write a short story. He'll think of all the rotten short stories he can lay hand to and make a short story like that.

DIANE: You were talking about the line between drama and melodrama. You know, there's another line between honesty and sentimentality.

GLADYS: That's a very tender one. The people who are mawkish, especially girls who are of about a B grade, of a tender nature, and a rather plain person, these girls are the hardest bunch, I think, to deal with in the world. They don't dare to have true feelings; so they have false feelings. I don't know. I always connect it with—my husband will say, please take away all those little china animals that are around the house. They were only invented to take the mind of the proletariat off its troubles. You know, Diane, I don't know how you can get rid of sentimentality. You can't go around and take somebody's paper and make large lines under it and say, "This is sentimentality," and have them say to you, "What does sentimental-ity mean," and you say, "That's false feeling, it's overdone feeling, it's feeling that goes too far for the amount of stuff that is there," because that destroys the person. I don't really know how to deal with sentimentality except to give it a B, and then in conference to say, "Look now. Was that the way it really was?"

Then there is the other thing. Sentimentality is not only false feeling or overdone feeling, it's unearned feeling; and it always supplies only one side of a situation. I mean you can't get sentiment-al about an old girl who has died if you say, "Look, she was a wonderful old girl. In fact, I remember how she used to take Gospel sayings and change them into sort of rural light works of her own. Why, she used to say, 'Cast your bread upon the water so it will come back cinnamon cake.' Or when the Salvation Army woman came around when she was picking up horse manure and putting it on the roses, and the lady addressed her and said, 'Madam, are you looking for the spirit of Jesus?' she said, 'Scarcely here.' She made 150 dolls once for the Hill City Community House. The little girl came to visit her to thank her for the dolls and left a doll of her own. The old girl said, 'You know, that's not a very good doll. You'd think at her age, she'd be able to do better.' She went to church every fifth Sunday, and I was angry at her one day out of every seven, and I loved her dearly one day out of every twenty, and I should have done more for her considering what awful fights she had with my grandmother in order to protect me when I was small." What I'm trying to say is if you get the whole damned thing, all levels of it—what was for, what was against; what was funny, what was sad; what was preposterous, what was to be taken for granted; what was grave, and what was just inventive—then it's like a handful of confetti. It's vari-colored, and you can't say anything against it.

Anybody who says, "I was right. I was one hundred percent right," is likely also to say, "I will shine before the throne of God and enter immediately into Heaven." And if you do, it must be a hell of a place to spend eternity because it's going to be terribly dull and terribly flat. I don't know. I think you get rid of sentimentality by thinking of life not as if it were a mirror in which certain images register themselves permanently with beautiful clarity, but as if it were a prism that keeps going round and round and keeps catching different facets of different images of different ways to see things—because anything that is many-leveled is never sentimentality. If a rose is one hundred percent beautiful—awful. Whatever creative powers were at work in the world knew enough not to make anything perfectly symmetrical.

There is a wonderful Japanese story about absolutes that I think I told some time ago in my Fiction Four class. The story goes along, with great sentimentality, about a young man who was out in the marketplace. He was a young man of great strength and great beauty, and he was looking among the goods in the bazaar for precious things. Suddenly he saw walking in front of him, but with her face turned and walking away, the most beautiful shoulders, the most beautiful heels. She began to go out of the marketplace and into the hills. He followed her and followed her and followed her, and she didn't turn around for hours. He followed her up and up and up to the top of the mountain. Then, just as the sun was setting, she turned her face around, and it had no features. It was as blank as an egg. It had no features because it was too damn perfect and the story teller knew that.

The most interesting thing about registering anything human is the infinite variety. Your Elly is preposterous and pitiable and despicable. Your Barnaby, you know, he's sad and droopy and lovable and hurt. Your central character—I'm only now going so far as I've read—is brave and wincing and cruel and kind and frightened, and he wishes he were dead, and he has to be alive, and he reaches out to live. As long as there are contradictions, there's no sentimentality. It's when, "God, that was utterly beautiful," "Lord, I was absolutely right," "She is a completely blessed memory," that there's no living with it. No living with it. A dead person about whom you can remember no flaw is the worst ghost that you can conjure out of the grave. The only people you can forgive who have gone dead on you are the ones whose flaws you can remember and smile.

Some of the most beautiful Japanese carvings I have ever seen were wood carvings of the ugliest toads you could imagine in the world. They're marvelous to pick up. The carving follows the knots in the grain of the wood, and they're wonderful to handle. The shape is beautiful, but they're ugly, ugly toads. And they're toads.

Another thing I always emphasize is in physical description. There is nothing in the world more boring and more deadly than evoking on the page a perfectly beautiful woman; nobody believes in that beauty. But if you give us a perfectly beautiful woman who has a little scar across here, a perfectly beautiful woman who has what one student in my Fiction Four had, a lovely, perfectly winsome face with one front tooth that is just about a tenth of an inch forward, it makes the whole face. Gives it a wittiness and delight. She has come to me half a dozen times and said, "Miss Schmitt, do you think that I should get this tooth replaced?" and I've said, "No. For God's sake no," and she said, "You know, I think you really like me." And the answer is, "Yeah, and partly because of that tooth."

Anything that is flawless is unthinkable—courageous young men who are always courageous, strong-minded men who are always strong-minded. I love to see a strong-minded man with a belly ache or a perfectly beautiful woman who has just encountered a drop of precipitation. There's room in the world for everything, and honest to God, you've just got to unmask your characters.

I would go so far as to carry the same principle a little further and apply it to literature. I am not of the school who believes that literature is an enshrined piece of human edicta that should be handed on to the people for enlightenment. I think it is one person's view of the world, and I do not think you really know that literature or really love that literature unless you see some flaws in that literature as well as the virtues in it. A perfect piece of literature would be almost as repellent as a perfect human being. And when a writer falls on his face, I don't see that it's any reason to exalt. But I do think it ought to be pointed out that possibly the school of criticism that makes it impossible for us to point it out without seeming to be just hideously rude, and maybe arrogant, is transcendental thought. That, I think, has been a rather bad influence on American literature and American attitudes altogether, to say nothing of one's being a great deal more arrogant to point out that when Shakespeare writes about tears he makes you sick at your stomach. Everybody has his flaws, and I think the approach to literature ought to be the same as the approach to people.

Fitzgerald, a great author. *The Great Gatsby,* a book that was carved out like a pocketed jewel and was flawed with one big flaw, Fitzgerald's own capacity to lie to himself about the existence of a glittering, shining light somewhere that he could never reach up to. And Fitzgerald to his last day had the same sort of image we have as children when we walk past lighted windows in other neighborhoods and we look up at them and think, there's the life—there's where the magic is. Not in me, not in my house, not in my friend's house, but up there in that unknown place is some light that I can never reach. And my life becomes your life. And everybody's life is pretty much like everybody else's, and besides, it's the only life we've got.

DIANE: In western civilization's tendency to categorize, I think we have the source of sentimentality.

GLADYS: It's one of the sources, certainly. As soon as you categorize, you begin to simplify. As soon as you begin to simplify, you sweeten out lines. As soon as you keep smoothing out lines, you can go to the point where you can take a person like Michelangelo, who is the most rough-hewn, impossible, knock-about, edgy, angry, wonderful human being in the world and turn him into some movie gallant in *The Agony and the Ecstasy.* You really have to work hard to do that, and that could only happen in the western simplification and categorization.

Beethoven, who in his last period wrote sublime material and very gnarled and eccentric material, in his middle period wrote a lot of material that completely embodies the eighteenth century sensibility, which has unfortunately passed over into sentimentality. There are certain themes and movements in Beethoven's concertos that eventually just make you sick at your stomach, especially if you've heard the real thing in the movements of the later period. He sings too easily in his middle period. After he came through a great deal of suffering and could sing on top of it, then maybe you could believe him.

LLOYD: Another problem of late is artificiality of style. Flaubert actually describes a woman's hat down to the glass bead to represent the dew on the flower. The passage was too perfect an image for me. It summed up craftsmanship, but it was so obvious. I was so conscious of Flaubert working and working and reworking it.

GLADYS: I know completely what you're talking about, Lloyd, and I think the only way you can guard against that—and I think we better start guarding against it—is to remember writing is only a way to get something across. It is a tool. It should be as clean, as beautiful, and as right as it can possibly be, but it's writing for a purpose, never for itself. As soon as you begin to say, "At this point in my novel, I will now stop. I will introduce a piece of still description," and you introduce a piece of still description, and you introduce the most beautiful piece of still description, the key word is, "I stopped." In other words, I deserted what I was doing. The thing, that device became more important to me than what I was really saying. Read such a thing as *Salammbo*. How many of you have read that Carthagenian novel? God. Turns your stomach inside out. Everybody dies there in the most exquisitely worded, beautifully balanced sentences. Perfectly horrible historical situation, and he treats it as if it were some kind of handsome jewel going back and forth in his hands. Really loathsome to experience. If you keep using writing as a tool, and you think, I want a word that gets the meaning that is in my head into his head, even if that's a cheap sentence, you won't be at fault. I mean, if you really want to write beautiful descriptions of women's hats or legs or any other thing, for all that matter, you can always still write them and you can cut them out afterwards and you can put other things in instead of description.

JOHN: Another comment on this twentieth century preciosity of style. A tragic example is the late Hemingway, where he latches onto imitating early Hemingway.

GLADYS: I thank you for bringing up Hemingway. In Hemingway, the style did become more important than the material. In the beginning, especially in the early short stories and the first two novels, Hemingway forged the style to serve the material. Then he absolutely became imprisoned in his style. It was almost as if he were too proud of what he had created. Thereafter, poor Hemingway got to the point where he could only write about such material as could be imprisoned in the style he had made for himself. Can you imagine a Hemingway story about an urban academic situation?

It's unthinkable. The style wouldn't work. It will work for violent action. It will work for heroic deeds. It will work for wild places. It will work for safaris; it will work for the bull ring. Eventually he had wrung it out and wrung it out and wrung it out until it became an impoverished edition of itself. I've often wondered if that was part of the reason why Hemingway, who was a great speaker of courage and of life, couldn't do what any blasted little clerk whom most of us know manages to do: live out the last years when the physical image begins to fail. There isn't so much pleasure to be found in bars. If you don't confine yourself, if anything is open to your art or to your thought, you run a much, much longer and much, much better chance of living a much, much longer and much, much more rewarding intellectual life. It's when you say, "I'm the type of man who," or "I write the type of sentence which. . . . " That eventually becomes so characteristic that it's exclusive, and I do think this happened to Hemingway.

Whoever would want to keep doing the same thing again? You'd have to be awfully desperate and also awfully self-mistrusting to want to write the same thing over and over and over. It would be like some pianist who could play only one concerto or one etude and would keep doing it and doing it. Or looking to play only etudes or concertos. That is a terribly limiting and sad thing to do. As the years go by, one is limited enough. One is limited in how much one eats and how long one stays out and how many books one can read. Why put unnecessary armors and limitations on yourself?

If you can't live as completely as you want to in this world, if you are a writer, you have the world of the imagination you can live in. If you've done nothing except slowly drain yourself until you're only imitating your own last work, which mocks your first work, you really have made a bad mess of yourself. I think that it's something that's happened more frequently in American literature than anywhere else. Think, for instance, of early Shakespeare historical plays, and then think of the middle plays, and then think of the last period plays. My God, it's just a wide vastness. It goes out and ripples into everlasting. No confinement there.

Shakespeare was confined only in the uses of the world for which he produced, which is another thing to touch on for a minute—the uses of the world for which we produce. There has been a good deal of thought that if you produce anything really good, nobody wants it or will buy it and care for it. It must necessarily be a rather second rate piece of art. The novel that is the really great novel of the week or the month is the one which nobody reads excepting six people in five departments: Harvard, Michigan, Cambridge, and so on and so forth. And this is the great, great novel because it is beyond the touch of common ordinary people: those who do such things as have children, nurse old ladies until they die, work for their bread and butter, and then come home and listen to people's troubles. Ordinary stuff like that, your work should be above. But when your work is above that, your work is uprooted. You have got in your hand one orchid, and it will live for a few years if it has good luck. A work is not necessarily despisable, or never has been until the 20th century, if it is a work which attracts human beings. My mother-in-law, who was a Russian Jewish girl, worked on a farm. She learned to read Russian herself. She was extremely poor. She did domestic work when she finished working on a farm. She was one of hundreds of people who walked ten miles in the freezing cold to go to the city of Minsk and stand in line for five or six hours in order to collect the monthly issues that brought her sections of Tolstoy's *Resurrection*. Does that mean Tolstoy's *Resurrection* was a rotten book? Far from it.

When Virgil walked into the arena before the games, everybody got up and yelled, "Hail, Virgil," loudly once and sat down. Does that mean Virgil was no good? When the cities of Pompeii and Herculaneum were preserved in lava, there were three things written on the walls: Praise to young gladiators, dirty jokes, and lines from Virgil. I don't think Virgil minded.

When El Greco's painting of Toledo was hung up and unveiled, all the population around came. Maids, farmer, petty artisans looked at it and said proudly, "There's my house. That's the way it looks under the sky when it looks that way." It doesn't mean El Greco was a rotten painter.

Once literature has become the property of nothing but academicians, nothing but the elite, the literature has lost its life. It is uprooted. Things have to be done to get the novel back into the world again. We worry too much about whether we are being esoteric, about whether we have a new look on things. What we've got to worry about is getting a little life back into prose literature, or the whole damn thing will die. Just perish away because it is slowly being uprooted, and not so slowly, at that.

The last great writers of novels that we've had were Hemingway and Faulkner. You figure out for yourself how many years ago that was, and you can see what kind of shape literature is in. Anybody you can think of writing now that has the stature and power of Faulkner and Hemingway? No one. No one. And Hemingway confined himself. Faulkner did manage a really lordly production of works, yet somehow managed to please the elite and very often the general reader.

By the way, Faulkner's short stories are really terrific. How many people here know Faulkner's short stories? You haven't read Faulkner if you haven't read his short stories. They're simpler, more direct perhaps, but a magnificent job. "Red Leaves," "Dry September," "A Rose for Emily." Just beautiful structure and also a haunting quality of humor. There are stories of Faulkner that you absolutely can't get out of your mind. I'm inclined to forget the names and situations in the novels and have to go back and reconstruct, but the stories, once you read them the more impressive they get.

DIANE: Do you see the effort of a number of contemporary writers, black or white, to use the language of the streets in novels as sometimes, if not always, a successful attempt to bring the novel back to Faulkner?

GLADYS: I wish I could say yes, but most of the younger writers who use the language of the street use it with affectation; and the language of the street is itself so compressed that they hardly have a language to write in. There is the trouble with the shrinking of language altogether. People don't talk to each other. They have certain hunks of terminology like "Yeah, man," or "Oh wow," or half a dozen phrases that seem to be current for signs. They don't really talk. If you can make that language grow, if you could make it expand somehow, I'd say, yes, absolutely, but I don't see any tendency to make it expand, to make it catch on.

PAULA: Can you give me hints on description of place? Dialogue. It seems I can write dialogue for days, but when it gets to description —and I know what I want to say in between the parts too—but the description sounded, you know, corny.

GLADYS: Description of place. I should say that in the current novel, Paula, nobody ever stops and gives a set description of place if he can possibly help it. He tries to work it in between. He does counterpoint on it. If you want to be modern—and I think, by the way, this is the best way to do it, too. . . . you don't say, "So and so walked into a large dining room with two buffets, one on each side, and some candlesticks and some glitter of crystal, so on and so forth. And then the maid said to him, 'Will you sit down, sir?'

and he sat down." What you do is: "Mr. So and So walked into a large, highly polished room. The maid said to him such and such. He sat down, being careful not to let his raincoat drip on the tapestried chair." And so they continue to talk a little bit here and a little bit there, and you keep it as scant as you possibly can. A great guy on description, by the way, is Henry James. He is so terribly interested in the development of character that he just naturally wedges in these little bits. What is that perfectly famous ghost story. . . .

VOICES: "Turn of the Screw."

GLADYS: Thank you so much. Boy, the brain is getting thin, too. There are two sentences in which he describes the dining room where the first vision of Quint at the window takes place. I'd love to be able to quote it. I can't. But go and look at that. Two sentences. I think it was "the cool polished mahogany and brass temple that was the dining room," and that's absolutely all. And at one point, "I had mended my gloves and thrown them down on such and such a chair," and that's all the evocation of place that you get.

The idea is to choose a sort of general description of place and then maybe fix it up with one sharp detail. You could describe this place. You'd say, "The unimpressive buff-colored light-drenched square of a room, the windows of which were so filthy that everything outside looked as if it were a vast orange fog." That's the way it appears to me at the moment. A generalized description, a detail.

A description of person works very well the same way. I think Thomas Mann is the best source for description of person. I think I told you about that marvelous description of his of a young man of military bearing who always stood very straight, whose ears stuck out very far on both sides. You take a general description, fill in one characterizing detail, and leave the rest to the reader's imagination because the reader likes to a certain degree to construct his own rooms, construct his own people. You don't have to give him much.

Okay? All right. We'll see you all. I'm beginning to think I'm going to miss you an awful lot when you're not around.

Out of Despair: *Sonnets for an Analyst*

Lois Lamdin

Gladys Schmitt once confessed that her reluctance to publish the sonnets written during her years of analysis had less to do with their revelatory nature than with her embarrassment at having couched those revelations in such an unfashionable form. But to those who knew Gladys, her work and her person, the sonnet form seems inevitable; it was the very nature of her style, her genius and her life itself that it must be firmly contained. Form was a bulwark against threatening chaos; if one's life and work were not to succumb to the ravages of time, despair and the aimless ringing of telephones, they must be rigidly structured.

I needn't dwell on the aspects of structure in Gladys' and Simon's lives: the "tea time" in the evening when they welcomed close friends, the breakfast rituals, the rigidly defined times for shopping, beauty parlors and reckoning up of accounts; the separation of academic preparation times from writing times; the schedule of books to be read and re-read; the formal entertaining, the strictly defined household roles, those scheduled Sunday afternoon hours when phones and doorbells went unanswered as they retired to bed for a few hours of God knows what.

It was this compulsively ordered existence that served as a defense against the demands of the mechanics of living, a dual career as teacher and writer, the social, financial, and physical exigencies, the disintegrating forces of love and despair.

All this may seem a cumbersome introduction to the sonnets, but it is essential to recognize that the passion for order that set the tone of Gladys' daily life carried into her creative life. In an interview in 1969 she said,

Lois Lamdin is Associate Dean at Empire State College—SUNY. She is interested in the British novel, the Victorians, the Jewish-American novel and individualized education. Her publications include articles on Malamud, Tennyson, Trollope and individualized education; and she co-edited The Ghetto Reader *and wrote a monograph on* Interpersonal Competencies.

The choosing of a strict form—of the strictest possible form—to impose on the rawest and most confused material would certainly be—. . . a push for order. (Interv., p. 6)

and

I believe art is form; I don't believe in formlessness. And it seems to me that the more chaotic and the more crazy and the more impossible and complex life is, then the more orderly, the more exquisite, the more capable of all sorts of stretching out to take in complexity art ought to be. (Interv., p. 34)

The demands of the sonnet, the constraints of length, rhyme and meter, were a natural medium for one who had, as a child, memorized whole sections of Shakespeare's sonnets and who had little sympathy for the random, the chance, the totally experimental, the "'we-don't-need-reason-any-more' kind of feeling about art" (Interv., p. 19).

But beyond her artist's feeling for the economy and order of the sonnet, how appropriate the form would seem for the analysand working not only during those fifty minute hours (another ritualistic form), but during the periods of intense introspection that followed, during the sleepless hours of the night, during dreams and fantasies, to sift through the debris of life, to arrange the flood of events and memories, the guilts and repressions of a lifetime into meaningful patterns. Thanks to the brevity of the sonnet, Gladys could work in manageable segments, exploring individual insights and recently exhumed materials without waiting until she could see their relation to the whole sequence. Each poem was individually crafted, complete in itself and true to itself.

Beyond the craftsman, the artistic intelligence was working on some other, possibly pre-conscious level, that governed the inter-poem connections, that moved not linearly but on a number of planes simultaneously. However, the work of the synthesizing intelligence would come later. During the actual writing, as images were selected, discarded, lines re-ordered, honed to a fine edge, the relentless editing process became part of the patient's as well as the artist's search for truth. The end couplet of the Shakespearean form provided a sufficient stop so that the poet could make interim statements: the truth of a particular moment, of a particular mood. Thus the progress of the analysis itself—the plungings in and backings off, the hesitations and negations and affirmations—each could be explored in turn and in isolation from the conflicting thoughts of yesterday.

Each poem thus stands alone, a complete work of art inviting serious explication, but each also takes on new hues and meanings when read in the sequence. For despite the richness of individual poems, the resonance, the full accomplishment of *Sonnets for an Analyst* cannot be fully experienced unless one has read all sixty-nine. It is then that the cross references, the image clusters, the incremental repetitions, the language patterns and thematic material can be apprehended as a whole that transcends its episodic creation.

New Critical edicts aside, it is useful to summarize the climate of Gladys Schmitt's life during the years when these poems were being written. Nearly sixty when she began writing them, she was honored as a teacher, but as a writer she had yet to receive the serious critical attention she knew she deserved. She had suffered a series of deaths in the family, her husband was just emerging from a serious emotional illness, physical problems plagued them both. Although her struggle out of poverty was over, the fruits of her financial security were less meaningful than she had hoped. Younger people were in the ascendancy both in her personal and professional life, and though she loved them and praised them generously, they must have made even more apparent to her the erosion of time. From her earliest years as the awkward child of a beautiful mother, she had never gotten over thinking of herself as a poor dried stick of a woman, and her need for fulfillment in love was largely played out in fantasy. Never having fully experienced motherhood (her niece Betty was ten when Gladys and Simon adopted her), she had embraced the grandmother role with a passion, but its joys were occasional and fraught with family tensions. A lifetime of depression had accumulated an unendurable weight on her soul when she finally began to see the analyst to whom these sonnets are addressed.

The sonnet sequence truly is *for* the analyst and about the processes stimulated by the analysis. In part the progress of the sequence depends upon the progress of the poet's relationship with the analyst, the shifting states of their interaction, the subtle choreography of the approaching, retreating, flirting and withdrawing as the tempo of their Freudian minuet plays now allegro, now adagio.

In the first sonnet, the poet assumes a classical patient stance, skeptical and challenging. As one who lives by the word, she is particularly skeptical of the language of analysis, of psychiatric jargon and its inadequacy to reality, its tendency to corrupt thought. The gauntlet is thrown down in the first line, "I do not buy your terminology." She goes on to equate the language that would reduce man to a set of Freudian phrases with the corruption of language that culminated in the atrocities of Auschwitz. Even more defensively, she immediately rejects the basic analytic myth, denying that "Oedipal" is an apt word to describe her relationship with her father. However, as though in an effort to anticipate him, she uses the analyst's language against herself to say derisively that her life is illustrative not of "charity" but of a "masochistic bind," just as her "chastity" is symptomatic of being "turned off, withdrawn, afraid." This quick shift to self-abasement is in part a rhetorical ploy, but also establishes a tone of self-denigration that continues throughout most of the poems and is an essential indicator of the nature of her depression.

But in a sudden shift in the last two lines, the skeptical facade collapses, and in the final couplet naked fear emerges.

> "They say the owl . . . " The girl's regressed, no doubt.
> "Oh, howl, howl, howl . . . " Listen! Old Lear is acting out.

Schmitt's submerged voice is heard in Ophelia's madness and in Lear's, as she suddenly confronts the possibility that she may in fact truly be insane. However, she deals with the fear ironically, adopting the psychiatrist's language as a defense against her terror. To say that Ophelia is "regressed" and Lear "acting out" is to combat the enemy with his own weapons.

For combat it is, as is clear in sonnet three which develops the image of the psychiatrist as hunter and she as helpless prey, afraid even to flee. His "planned face," in which memories are illuminated, promises pain, and she contemplates wrenching free (discontinuing analysis) before she is further wounded, but terrifyingly, she has already lost control of the situation.

> Stay? Run? All reason's gone, the world's askew
> When hunted says to hunter, "What am I to do?"

Again, the classic patient, she insists on the reality of her vision; having "no use for dreams" (7), she tries to view the analyst dispassionately. She remembers when she wept in his office and was handed a paper handkerchief, suggesting his sympathy is out of that same box. The situation of paying for the analyst's support, compassion, pity, even love, is a constant in the poems and difficult to resolve. The commercial nature of their transaction, "You hear because I pay you" (19), is a stumbling block as the transference gets under way. She thinks of him from dawn to twilight; he thinks of her when she pays her bill.

> Money—except to give away—is shit.
> And money's all you want and have of me. (19)

The words "ghostly gigolo," elsewhere applied to fickle sleep, here describe the psychiatrist and connote her shame at taking part in a commercial transaction. She is bribing this gigolo that he may view her naked soul; however, he must remain "ghostly" because the nature of their intercourse precludes the physical. In the following poem, which continues the thought processes of number nineteen, she examines her own role as an academic. Is she a teacher/whore as he is psychiatrist/gigolo? She protests that what she gives to and feels for her students goes beyond what she is paid for.

> It's not for dollars that I dare to pour
> My naked heart into "Byzantium" (19)

Perhaps he, like she, does not lay his "hand upon one head in order to be paid."

A major turning point in the analyst/analysand relationship occurs in sonnet eighteen when she begins to recognize his power in a positive sense as a will moving through her, an unseen undertow, moving "through my darkest dark." Apparently she has begun to believe in the connection between her dreams and the therapy; "Sleep works your purpose. Nightmares bear your mark." The poem, based on undersea imagery, has itself the flow of the tides that convey the unconscious, shift the landscape of the deep. She pays homage to her new understanding of his power to release her from old constraints in a magnificent sestet:

> Some wrecked intention with a salt-sheathed mast
> Shuddered and fell apart, for you were there.
> Lost coins turned over; ivory ribs heaved bare
> Out of stirred sea-anemone. At last
> A buoy-bell broke the dream and I awoke
> And said . . . But then, who was it—I or you—who spoke?

The final question, "Who was it—I or you—who spoke?" strikes a new note: her inability to separate the processes of her mind from his, her recognition that he has penetrated the core of self.

Nevertheless, the merging of identities is temporary. As the relationship takes on the characteristics of the love affair, it must also be subject to the terrors and heartbreaks inherent in love affairs. Conditioned throughout life to expect rejection, she already foresees the cold ending of the analysis, "the end of this limp comedy" (25), when, like other patients before her, she will have become boring to him; he will salve her pride by "explaining how you could not love me: sure,/If you could love you could not work a cure," and she will say she understands, will try to convince him that she doesn't "confuse refusal with rejection," though even in prospect the pain is palpable.

The inherently paradoxical nature of the psychiatrist's role is explored in number twenty-six which deals with "the interim," that period prior to his final rejection of her, in which he sits poured in Freudian cement "like patience on a monument, . . . Dispensing mercy by the tick of clocks." Again, the insistence on the exploitative nature of their commerce. Although he seems geniunely dedicated to healing her "bitter scar," she also fears he may be "prone to show it in [his] seminar." The paradoxical images build up. He is:

> Soul-naked, yet well buttoned in a coat,
> Warm like a friend, yet not at all a friend,
> Strong to the end, yet eager for the end,
> Close as the skin that's on me, yet remote.

And finally two oxymorons, "cozy distance" and "gregarious solitude," epitomize the antithetical nature of his stance. The poet is compelled to remind herself that she must be wary of this paid friend, who has become so necessary to her. The exploration of the paradox is a way of mitigating anticipated pain by dealing with it before the fact, and thus avoiding the ultimate despair which she foresees at the end of treatment.

To this point in the sonnet sequence, though Gladys has begun to respond to the analyst in positive ways, he has not yet made significant inroads on her depression. Then, in number twenty-eight, he has apparently said something that releases her anger, turning her from a human being into a vengeful walking corpse. Not yet prepared to deal with such anger, she is almost destroyed by it. The rhythms of the poem quicken, the language takes on a mechanical brutality.

> My speech is mangled by my grinding jaws,
> My fists are hammers and my fingers claws.
> . . .
> I hate, I hate, and nothing is exempt.

Following the onslaught of anger, she considers withdrawal, silence, as a way of avoiding him; she could, after all, simply refuse to answer, lie blank and mute; she could assume the dominant role through her very passivity.

> Baffle and craze him with that woman's mind,
> That woman's soul, that spurious mystery
> Which all men want and no man ever had of me.

She could, thus, reduce their relationship to the limited, enigmatic relationships she had previously known and circumvent the pain and hurt she now knows he can reveal. But the mood is transient, a momentary defensive posture, because in number thirty-one his attempt to relieve her guilts, his "insistent voice" coming through a shroud, at least evokes the question of whether she *can* awaken. Can she begin to hold up her bludgeoned head again through recognition that her guilt is shared and "the slaying's stain/Lies more upon the slayer than upon the slain?"

Sonnet number thirty-seven marks a glorious surrender, an invitation to the psychiatrist to perform his magic. The controlling image is the psychiatrist as the "soul's geologist," invited to dig down through the "clay of fear," the obsidian of anger, the black diorite of hunger, down, down, down to the core of "red need that can be slaked no more." Here, the poet's self has abandoned the earlier resistance and lies passive, a "layered lie/That other men call 'she' and I call 'I'." There is almost a note of exultation in the invitation to mine the depths of this self, an opening up, a surrender. The note in the last line of the self observed as opposed to the self itself is an abandonment of the tightly closed off persona, a recognition that that other self which men perceive may, in fact, be susceptible to the reality testing of another, may yield up secrets which will free the self that "I call I."

Number thirty-seven indeed seems a watershed, for there is a clearly discernible turn from that point, not only in their relationship, but in the progress of the analysis. She recognizes the inevitable sexual undercurrents, as when she speaks of carrying the new insights and strengths he has given her to the marital bed, ashamed of this strange infidelity in which her orgasms are "traitorous." Yet she recognizes that the analyst must avoid overt sexual response if he is to be successful. "Your deep uncaring care" acknowledges the professional concern that steers clear of eros.

An even more significant breakthrough is chronicled in sonnet forty-three where his laughter at one more in a series of her mea culpas arouses a response in her which smashes through the depression.

> Smoked glass smashed, a grimy pane and whorled
> Cracks, and I sight an undistorted world.

For the first time, she is able to see through his eyes and realizes that she is not damned but possibly only "amiably daft," and is able to say, with an echoing light-heartedness that is all the more striking for the anger that has preceded it,

> I like you well
> Convivial priest, light-hearted harrower of hell.

That the laughter has been cleansing is apparent in the following poems, in which the depression, even when it returns, is unaccompanied by the earlier mistrust and anger against the agent of revelation. Indeed, in sonnet forty-five, celebrating the uniqueness and complexity of the human brain, the meanest of which "houses a miracle," she finds the distinguishing quality of her own mind is that "you [the psychiatrist] took a room, you lived in it a space."

Anxiety about the end of treatment, which she both wills and does not will, becomes enmeshed in sonnet fifty-three with the end of other relationships, when the memory of the loved one's voice went first. Thus her "I cannot hear you speak" presages yet another loss. She wishes to but cannot quite deny the implication that her inability to hear him is in a sense a death wish, one that counters her conscious desires.

> Needing you, could I wish to see you going?
> Living within you, could I wish to see you dead?
> If this is of my willing, kill my will;
> My will's my enemy; it wills me only ill.

However, the implicit agony of the questions in the first two lines is somewhat altered by the final couplet in which internal rhyme and word play provide a counterpoint to the seriousness of the message. One senses that at yet another level the questions have already been answered, that the end of treatment, when it comes, will be experienced as not death but growth.

In some moods the poet is still angered by the analyst's objectivity, seeing it as sterile, but she has accepted, though not without cost, the reality that their intercourse must be verbal, that the thought must be the act, for neither the fee she pays nor her need gives her the right to his body. Thus, the rest of the poems in the sequence take the style of the relationship for granted; what remains to be worked out can be accomplished without reiterating earlier, more worrisome questions. In the jargon which she so resisted, the transference seems to have been resolved.

The relationship with the analyst could not, of course, be divorced from earlier relationships and was to some extent patterned after them. Primary among these relationships, primary to Gladys to the day she died, was that with her husband Simon. Simon is as central to the sonnets as he was to Gladys' life. She had rarely spent more than a few hours away from him in the thirty-five years of their marriage. Theirs was a practical and intellectual symbiosis. They shared her career, their friends, their pride in the home that she bought with the proceeds of *David the King,* their passion for order. But despite the "twenty-odd years I've lain in the bed I made" (1), she feels as she enters treatment that he is "a stranger now, and I alone" (2), that she wants from him compassion, not sex. She realizes that in her depression she has used him by connecting him with her deaths and her losses, that for all their closeness, she has groped for him where he was not, and now is ashamed

> to make such use
> Of what, if I had never fallen sick,
> Would still have touched me—yes, and sweetly, to the quick. (4)

The time leading up to and immediately after Simon's emotional breakdown in 1962 had been especially difficult, and for the first time since their marriage, Gladys was beginning, in analysis, to recognize and deal with the ambivalences of their relationship— her resentment at carrying much of the burden of their lives, the total intertwining of love and hate—but yet the impossibility of their separating. And, a real revelation, she now realized that he shared her ambivalence. The following lines from sonnet forty-one provide the objective correlative of their symbiosis (as well as an example of the nature imagery that is so basic to the sonnets):

> If thirty years have fused two vines in one,
> To separate them is to rip and mangle
> In hopes of salvaging a limp green tangle
> That's doomed to wilt at the first touch of the sun.

Certainly it was unhealthy to be so interdependent, but surely at this late date they could not survive separately. Trapped in her wish that he were dead and her fear that he might die, she realizes that he shares—yet another sharing—the same feelings.

> . . . more shame to take his warmth when he
> Will wake an hour from now in the same fright for me. (41)

156

However, if old rages at Simon have died, her hatred and fear of her mother-in-law have not. "That fierce preposterous woman/Who bore and mauled the one I thought was mine" (33) is still living with her, though dead, and still compelling Simon to mould Gladys in her hateful image. Simon has continued since her death to look for the mother in the wife, laid that ancient mask on Gladys and dealt with her in pre-patterned behaviors more appropriate to the son than to the husband. In his own groping back toward the womb, he has confused their identities, blaming Gladys for his mother's lovelessness. Gladys knows that she bears not the slightest resemblance to that mother-in-law for whose sins she has suffered.

> She raged, I fed stray cats in the back yard;
> She struck for blood and I filed down my claws.
> No, it is cruelty, it is harsh excess
> To beat a cringing dog as if she were a lioness. (34)

The relationship with Simon is, for a while at least, enmeshed in that with the analyst. In sonnet forty-eight the conflict between Simon and the analyst is embodied in a gardening metaphor that relates back to the third man in this trinity, her father. Simon is "he who clips and weeds," the tireless, obdurate critic whose editing has largely defined his role in her life. But now this editing, this "pruning," goes counter to the analyst's search for the patterns of her life in "tangled hopes and twisted needs." Simon has been rejecting as superfluous in art just that material that is richest for psychiatric exploration; and she, also the compulsive editor, with "incriminating scissors" in her head, conspires for a time with her husband against the "green chaos" that would be so fecund a source of psychoanalytic insights.

In their marriage the relentless editing had excised passion, tamed their love to a domestic, emotional and intellectual interdependence. This restrictiveness is captured in sonnet forty-nine in the image of the married couple drawing the draperies against the storm. But in both forty-eight and forty-nine, the wildness, the emotional lushness of an earlier time, perhaps a different lover, is remembered in the sestet. In forty-eight it is the "sweet/Season of May" and in forty-nine it is the

> herds of god-bred colts
> Whinnying down the wind, wild wants laid bare.

The analysis works to release these carefully expunged memories, to allow her to return to an earlier time when she and a lover were

"Standing, drenched mouth to mouth, among torn peonies."
Indeed, it is the memory of passion that is most painful and perhaps
most crucial, for in remembering former passions she must also
admit to current and long-standing frustrations.

This growing ability to face and even accept the emotional barren-
ness of her marriage controls the movement of sonnet fifty-four
which is, for the sonnet sequence at least, the final word on her
marriage. Here the structure is chronological, a perfect synthesis of
form, imagery and theme. The changing seasons and verb tenses
and moods, each expressed in a botanical object, show how the
understanding that Simon did not love her, could not love her,
would not love her and never loved her would have affected her
in the different seasons of life. The April bud penetrated by that
fact would have disintegrated into the spring mud; the August
flower would have "decomposed within the hour"; the burr of
autumn would have discharged its unready seeds. But in the winter
of her life (and here the plants give way to the unadorned "I")

> He never loved me, and the day arrived
> When I was old and dry, and knew it, and survived.

She has finally reconciled herself to Simon's lack of warmth, the
deprivation that had tortured her when she was younger and been a
constant source of anguish throughout most of her adult life.

The reconciliation motif is less obvious in those poems about her
family. Although Gladys' conversation frequently ran to reminiscences of her childhood, and stories of her mother and father were
an important part of her repertoire, the parents play a minor role
in the poems. Despite the rejection of the term "Oedipal" in the
first sonnet, her identification with her father is clear; he "lies
under dirt and snow" (1) as does half herself. Indeed, she speaks of
her physical resemblance to him "Who made me out of wanting,
slime, and air,"/Whose uncouth beak and hollow cheeks I bear/
Ungraciously." Thinking of him now dead, she identifies her
approaching old age with his: "My autumn knows his winter, scents
my own" (8). But the mourning for her father is not dwelt upon; it is
in his nurturing aspects that she primarily remembers him. He is
recalled as the gardener whose orange and yellow marigolds gar-
landed a bridal couple, and who even in death continues his gardening function by enriching the soil. Indeed, the pervasive nature
imagery of the sonnets may be seen as a continuance of the father
in the daughter. Once, in her waking dream, her father, now among

the dead, fails to recognize her, but this seems to be, in a perverse way, a sign of the progress of the analysis, for as he goes into the void, not raising "his workworn hand to greet his child" (39), she knows that his lack of recognition must mean that she has been cured of her earlier unhappiness, "of the leprous sore/By which he knew [her] once." (39).

The only references in the sonnets to her mother, that beautiful but rejecting presence, are in the dream sequence (21-23)* in which she remembers the three Russian dolls within dolls her mother gave her on the occasion of her brother's birth. Indeed, the primal family constellation is here: father, mother and brother. She, who was given that "one present and three presents," dreams of a wet Venice where she is invited to see the holy dead beside a curious shrine of cedarwood. Though it is raining, she draws into her nostrils a dry scent, "Parched petals, powdered incense, spices, wine—" and inside the church that, like the Russian dolls, held another and another, finds in the aisle between each two (churches, presumably), a Brother (the familial and theological work side by side here). The third church, which she cannot enter but from whose windows curl that dry scent, is like the cedarwood shrine, the womb, the mother, the gift giver, who is represented in the dream poems by the scents of cedarwood, dry brown sachet and sandalwood.

> No blossom-heavy, bee-inviting tree
> Spread such a memorable scent as she, (22).

"Dog-tired, dog-cold, dog-thin," she yearns to rest her head against that warm maternal breast, but she cannot re-enter that glowing womb, become a doll within a doll. The fire imagery of the sonnets is here a "gold fire of love" (23) with a dry scent that sweetens all the world (21).

What references there are in the rest of the poems to her mother and father are oblique, veiled, though the image patterns of flame (mother, love, passion) and of gardening (father, nurturing, natural) clearly have their origins and derive their emotional force from childhood memories.

The order of the poems in the sequence is, with a few exceptions, the order in which they were written and thus truly chronicles the poet's emotional progress as the accretion of insights and epiphanies achieved through analysis move her on the long journey from

---

*In a 1969 interview, Gladys referred to these as number 20-22; either she or Simon subsequently re-ordered them.

despair to acceptance. The despair of the earlier poems is palpable and unrelenting. I have written of the sonnet as appropriate to Gladys' passion for form but it is equally appropriate to her sense of imprisonment at the time she began seeing the analyst. She writes early in the sequence of the sky as "the shut lid of my sarcophagus" (5). Trapped in a depression from which neither her possessions nor her friends nor her talents can free her, she remembers feeling shut away, imprisoned, when as a child she was punished by being sent to her room "only with dolls and glass-eyed animals" (16). Even all these years later, the lines from Matthew, "I was in prison and ye visited me," bring tears to her eyes as she remembers that earlier deprivation. As an adult she is still trapped, imprisoned in her depression, in her marriage, in her memories of the dead, in relationships and patterns and obligations and old guilts. The recurrent torments of migraine are a physical manifestation of imprisonment; she feels shut within her head with the jiggling aura and the terrible pain and nausea, with the memories of sins both committed and imagined.

Sonnet thirteen, perhaps the nadir of her depression, a true dark night of the soul, catalogues the horrors of the universe, progressing from the macrocosm, the stars' senseless colliding, to the poisoning of the atmosphere, to the mindless deaths of animals, the racial wars, and finally to the microcosmic "clot that clogs an artery/ Engenders slobbering insanity." Even the process of analysis itself seems more demanding than she can bear. "Let me alone. I'm sick, I'm tired, I'm old" (15). And in a slightly different use of Frost's imagery, referring to the passions of her younger years, she laments, "I've died by fire three times. Please let me die of cold."

From a vision of such sustained misery, only sleep offers release, and that "ghostly gigolo" is courted avidly with seconal. Each night becomes a small death, a flirtation with finality, "Barbiturate rest presaging ultimate rest" (2). The intimations of suicide throughout the poems are made explicit late in the sequence when she runs through a retrospective litany of suffering, saying she has swallowed such things as holy wafers, defeat in love, critical indifference to her writing, deaths, loss of passion, "the mindless chaos of the universe," and wonders why, having suffered so much, she "cannot take this small/Pink heap of twenty tasteless Seconal" (65). That she can ask the question suggests that there may be an answer—a basic life-bound, life-seeking reality toward which she has been groping and which has stayed the hand with the pills.

Between sonnets twenty-seven and twenty-eight occurs the most dramatic turn in the sequence. Twenty-seven is an artfully sustained moan. She is merely going through the motions of life.

> Thinking now only of the end of it—
> How will I die and wherefore have I been?— . . .
>
> Now that love's gone, with sun and eyes put out,
> I plumb such primal dark as was before
> My mindless forebears heaved themselves ashore.

But then, something the analyst says releases a burst of anger, and the depression suddenly gives way to sheer rage. The force of her anger is overwhelming, terrifying and revolting, befouling even the holiest memories, but it is also cleansing and has the effect of relieving the depression. Immediately following this most powerful of poems, memories of her dead are thrown into the conflagration of her rage, leaving her past in ashes. This time the fire is neither the golden flame of mother love nor the heat of passion, but an angry, destructive fire that, for the time at least, obliterates the past, leaving only minimal clues, mere phrases, "She sang . . . He wept . . . We spoke . . . " (29).

From this meagre beginning, these mere scraps, she must refashion her world. First she must deal with a lifetime of guilt, must recognize that it makes no difference "Who bears the blame—forsaker or forsaken" (31), that it matters little who wins, who loses; the collision of two ships or two souls is an accident about which no value judgment must be made. For a while this abnegation of moral responsibility seems to lead back to an age when "wolves are padding up the avenue" (38), but as the depression lifts she recognizes that civilization survives despite mankind's dark, unconscious wishes. Man can still walk in the dark city and come back "Penis and purse and mortal skin intact" (44).

However, before she could approach reconciliation with her past, there was one more relationship that Gladys had to work through in the sonnets as in the analysis, and that was the relationship with God. Indeed, of all the losses she chronicles, of youth, love, family, hope, this may be the most profound.

Gladys denied having any formal religious belief, and indeed said she had "never decided God is alive or God is dead—never felt that through" (Inter., p. 9), but for the woman who wrote these poems God was certainly a presence, even in His absence. In one of the early sonnets, she remembers being told by her Lutheran grandmother that her "puny lies could plague my dying Lord" (11), and being plunged into self-loathing. For a child for whom pity had been a primal feeling, to be responsible for the pain of God "turned our kitchen into hell/And set me naked at its hissing core" (11). The sonnet that immediately follows is a childhood memory of the safe, clean Lutheran church, the varnished woodwork, the clean carpet and the squares of sunlight. This benign vision suddenly gives way as the child notices "a vent cut out to heat the nave" through which the cellar shows. In that vent she has a sudden vision of death, lying beneath a world that only *seems* clean and safe. This unbidden knowledge, this certainty of death, sends the child spinning into a void; the Bible becomes "a lie to soothe a fool," and the child, having lost God, is alone in a universe of terror. Sonnet thirteen, discussed earlier, moves away from the child's perspective to the adult's, but it is a catalogue of the horrors that occur on an earth in which there is no plan and in which the "no-God does not hear."

Though from the evidence of these poems, God seems to have died early for the poet, the imagery and the passions remain God-obsessed.

> I am God's dray-horse, whom He has forgot.
> Winded, in blinders—yes, and terrified
> As if His whip were biting through my hide— . . .
> Heavy the scrap-iron of His former wrath.
> Filthy the rags of His old mercies. (50)

She is still, over fifty years since she first questioned God's existence, still in thrall to the old terrors, guilts. A religion has died, but no new Word has come, or if it has, God's dray-horse* hasn't heard it and "must go down as His old Law goes down," not believing but grieving for her lack of belief and still tied to the anguish if not the promise of religion. "Bereaved that I am not bereft" (52), she is loathe to give up even the pain that stands between herself and utter nothingness.

One way of viewing the entire sonnet sequence, and it is a way that leaves ample space for a multitude of complexities, is to see it as chronicling the overwhelming depression of a life spent mourning

---

*The dray-horse image also has connections to the way in which Gladys envisioned her role in marriage. I remember her teasing but bitter aside one evening as her husband extolled her latest literary success. "Yes, Simon's proud that his squaw can carry more wood than your squaw."

His passing, summoning the "grace to grieve/Without the drugs of self deception." And indeed, if the final poem in the sequence is to be seen as some sort of a resolution, partial though it is, how sad that resolution: the poet, lamenting on her knees, "A nothing keeping watch with nothingness" (69), the one soul who has stayed to mourn, singing *Te Deum* into the void.

But lest that final vision seem too unrelievedly grim, it must always be remembered that the soul who stayed to mourn undoubtedly sent a few obscenities into the void along with those *Te Deums*. For all the anguish, the bereavements, the losses that the poems chronicle, the poet never completely relinquishes her sense of the ridiculous or her horror at the merely sentimental.

Consider the wit of the line about man's ability to walk in the dark city and come back "Penis and purse and mortal skin intact." In the alliterative pairing of the male sex organ and a receptacle for money, the Freudian double entendre, the abrupt change of tone, lie a key to that quality in the sonnets that consistently brings them back from their perilous closeness to bathos. Certainly the material dredged up in analysis could have tempted the poet to a continual emotional orgy. How easy to wallow in grief, the seductions of despair. But always there is the poet's other voice, the voice of saving wit, that refuses finally to take herself or anyone else too seriously. That wit is an astringent restorative that gives her the strength every so often to back off from the *sturm und drang,* to take an ironic, even satiric look at the universe and her rather insignificant place in it. Thus it is that she can think enviously of lucky Eve whose Adam had no mother; thus it is that after so much suffering over the lack of love, she can draw back and see the physical act of sex as "preposterous" (61).

> Entirely too much is made of it
> That any two agree in any weather
> To fit their gross and rebel parts together.

There is yet another voice in these poems, a missing voice—the analyst's. One can almost hear him at times in echoes of the poet's responses, but he is just out of earshot, distanced by the filtering mechanism of her psyche. He seems to have preserved a therapeutic distance, but one wonders, was he never seduced beyond the boundaries of his role, never tempted to forego disinterested observation for passionate participation? We know that once, at least once, he laughed, and we can hope that he may even at times

163

have wept. But if he actively intervened, that intervention is not recorded. We trust that his journey with Gladys through the ashes of her past was recognized as a privilege; that the room he took for a time in her brain gave him a lasting taste of the richness of the imaginative process; that these poems are recognized as a priceless gift to the Son of Hippocrates who couldn't really have left "contagious mortal care outside" (64).

CONSIDER THE GIRAFFE

Gladys Schmitt

It was precisely the right day for going to the zoo. "Precisely," like "asinine" and "intolerable," was one of her mother's words. Her father's were thicker and harder to find in the dictionary—"antediluvian," "agrarian," "bourgeoisie." Only these words and the conversations draped around them were permanent things. Everything else—furnished apartments, jobs, cities, rage, and tenderness—shifted from one month to the next. During last year she had been in the fourth grade in three different places, and knew that it was no use growing fond of the view from any window, the voice of any schoolmate, or the leaf shadows around any bed. Tomorrow or the day after tomorrow it would be necessary to be up and going again. The beloved four-poster would be lost; the ivy plant would stay behind on the abandoned windowsill. Only the conversations, thrown with differing degrees of success at different groups of people, were the same.

Anyhow, it was precisely the right day for going to the zoo.

There was enough sun to make you really want the cream of soda, and enough wind to dry the sweat on your forehead. The path was covered with jingling bits of light. The air parted the boughs and streamed down, and if you closed your eyes imaginary fingers stroked your hair. Here and there a maple tree, eager for autumn and yellow before the rest, broke upon you like an earthly sun. The caterpillar lay sleeping, curled in his cocoon on the bark, and you walked softly, not wanting to disturb his winter sleep. The park was beautiful enough; the park was a full week's share of loveliness. And the park was only a starter, like apple juice before a company dinner. After the park came the zoo.

Keeping far behind her father and mother, keeping out of the bluish shadow that trailed behind them on the walk, she thought how this holiday was a kind of miracle. Last night the zoo or anything pleasant had been out of the question. *They* had had one of their fights, screaming at each other in the midnight quiet of the apartment, so loudly that some neighbor had opened a window and

167

shouted, "For God's sake!" They had still been fighting, hoarse now and in hissing whispers, when she fell asleep in the living room on the couch. But she had wakened in the muffling blackness that comes to unfamiliar rooms before daylight, and they had not been fighting *then*. A change, perceptible as a change in weather, had taken place. It was disturbing to waken to it, like wakening under February blankets to the thick, moist warmth of spring. Sounds, their sounds, were being made behind the bedroom door, small squeaks and bursts of laughter, soft inside sounds, like cats gurgling after food. She knew then that they had made friends again. Not as she and her playmates made friends, taking hands in the sight of the sun, but in some dark and terrifying way not possible in daylight—a business of the night.

Even though he had said that the biscuits were antediluvian and she had found the coffee intolerable, their truce had lasted through breakfast. "A magnificent day—magnificent," he had said, turning from the window and giving his wife a smart slap on the thigh. "What do you say! Shall we take Francie to the zoo?"

All morning they had been royally kind. They let her wear her scarlet jumper streaked with rabbits' hair. That gave her some color, her mother said; a good clear red seemed to take the straw-iness out of her hair. Yes, said her father, more becoming all round—absolutely; not so much like a bag of bones. And now they had forgotten her entirely, which was even better. She jumped across a mossy log and could not feel her bones at all. She was smooth and all of one piece, like the sleek chipmunk racing down the lawn. She licked the last sweetness of the cream of soda from the corners of her lips, and whistled to herself.

First they went to see the hippopotamus who lived quiet like a lump of earth in a sky-green swimming pool. She could not tell why she liked him; he was really very ugly with his muddy, patchy skin and his little eyes; he blew large bubbles and had an amazingly big backside. Still, she thought she could have stayed for hours leaning her cheek against the rail and staring at the brown blob in the green water. He looked like Theodora's uncle. There was something peaceful about him. He never went anywhere. He stayed and stayed. Maybe he liked to open his eyes down there in the watery dark and see the same rough spots on the cement every day. Maybe . . .

"The Church of England to a T," her father said. "T. S. Eliot can always be depended upon to produce the perfect simile, the simile more factual than fact, more true than truth."

"Precisely," said her mother. "But don't you think she looks a little like Emma Fitzsimmons, too?"

She sighed over her own ignorance. She had made another blunder; she had taken a she for a he. The hippopotamus became what it had been in the beginning—a sexless chunk of mud, something indefinite enough to be like an English cathedral and Emma Fitzsimmons at the same time. They walked away, and she trailed after them without looking back at the little, stupid eyes.

They went to the front of the main building where the cages were, and she followed them with an old resignation. They were like that—she had been to other zoos with them in other cities—they always wanted to spend most of the time looking at the fierce ones, the ones behind bars. Afterwards they were too tired for her animals, the gentler ones, the jittery monkeys, the shy skittish zebras, the giraffes with the seeking eyes. This particular zoo had a new pair of black leopards. At the breakfast table they had talked about that. There was thunder somewhere in the line of cages, and she could tell by their eyes that they hoped it came from one of these black leopards, that somehow it would be more precious to them if it happened to be a black leopard's roar.

The insides of all the cages had an ancient, barren, Biblical look. Each of them had the same gray stone steps and the same stone-gray shadows. Flies could come in to sit on the tiger's moist nose and the lion's thick paw, but there was no way for the sunlight to get inside. These cages were vastly disheartening, like pictures of ruins. She kept thinking of something she had heard somewhere about lions creeping restlessly over a desert place where an old, old city had once been—a city with a wild name—Tyre, Nineveh, Babylon?

In the smoky grayness of the cage the soot-black leopards paced round and round, hissing with a noise like steam and glaring at people with their pale moonstone eyes. Her mother and father stayed as close to the cage as possible. They leaned on the railing and answered the dark creatures stare for stare. But she lagged behind in the shade of a kindly boxwood hedge and tried to think of pleasant matters: how fine the cream of soda had been, how clean the sky was, how red her jumper looked in the sun.

The roar *had* come out of those sleek and sinewy necks. Now they began it again, soft and gurgling at first, then stronger, more like a monstrous whine. She shivered and retreated against branches. The Bible had certainly gotten into the cage somehow; she saw the

Devil twice, black and lithe and terrible, springing up on lean haunches, clawing at the bars.

"Primitive!" her father said. "The primal evil. In the beginning was Lucifer."

And her mother nodded and said, "Precisely. Yes, indeed."

But that would not be enough for her mother to say. Before they ·could leave this cage, before the pale Devil's eyes could be blotted out by some softer, more sorrowful animal stare, her mother would have to find something else, something clever. Today there was no war between them, and he would wait until she had said her say.

Meanwhile some change, disturbing and disturbingly familiar, took place behind the black bars. The leopards stopped clawing at the grating, they eased their long bodies langorously down; they paced back and forth in opposite directions, passing each other, brushing briefly against each other's sides. Their heavy paws beat softly on cement. They hissed whenever they met, but, moving apart, they made remembered noises in their throats, gurgling sounds that belonged in the middle of the night.

"Yes . . . " the mother said, and stretched her shoulders and turned her head from side to side.

"Ah . . . " said the father, smiling with a cold, knowing mouth.

The child, watching from the hedge, knew that this wisdom between them was a secret and had to do with he-ness and she-ness; the black leopards were a he and a she; their quarrel was over, and the whole park was about to become thick and damp with a nameless thing; day was to be turned inside out with a business of the dark.

Some of the other mothers and fathers made loud conversations and began to push their children toward a low building, a delightful place where you could see Malay sun bears with crew haircuts, and raccoons hung upside down. The path looked abandoned and tawdry now, cluttered with candy wrappers and the limp ends of ice cream cones. Only the three of them stayed behind in this emptiness, watching the two black Satans, the he and the she, at their angry tryst behind the bars.

Fear drove her back into the hedge, so that the branches crackled against her face. She wished to God that she might close her eyes, but she could not close her eyes. The creatures lunged at each other, collided in midair, and fell in a wriggling heap. Their mouths were hissing and drawn back; in the undulating mass of fur, you could see the whiteness of their teeth and the redness of their gums. One of them leaped at the other, buried his teeth in a black neck, soiled the clean day, the bright park, the whole world with throaty night-sounds. . . .

"Oh, no!" she said.

Her mother called casually over her shoulder, "Don't be silly, Frances, they're only playing, they're doing that for pleasure."

"Shall we go along now?" her father asked. "I believe the show's over. I conclude the female's not in the mood for that particular variety of activity this afternoon."

Her mother dawdled, thoughtful, remote, still waiting for a cleverness.

One leopard came to the edge of the cage and thrust his sticky nose between the bars, into a slant of sun. The nose was not so terrible as it had seemed in shadow; it was really more brown than black; small, darker underpatches showed through.

The mother smiled. "A bad dye-job, that nose," she said. "Doesn't it look exactly like those figured curtains that Mrs. Moss had done over?"

He laughed and said, "Absolutely. Yes, indeed." And they turned to tell her it was about time to be getting on.

By the time that they had seen the lion and condors and had waited for twenty minutes to see whether the peacock would scream, she began to think it would be better not to visit any of the other animals; she began to wish that she could go straight home. It was true that she had wanted particularly to see the giraffe. One of her teachers in Cleveland had said that he was a very tame animal who liked people and ate nothing but green leaves. Still, he would probably not like her; she did not like herself any more; she was covered with a sick, chilly sweat, and her knees felt watery and tired.

But they were in such a good humor. They had decided to have supper in a restaurant close by, and they were not hungry as yet, and it would be utterly stupid to run home. Didn't she want to see the giraffe? Hadn't she said so this morning at the breakfast table? Well, look, there will be plenty of time to rest before supper. And here is a bench right in front of the giraffe's cage, and isn't that fortunate, and now all of us can sit down. . . .

For a long time she did not look at the giraffe. He was there somewhere, behind a wire fence in a small, sandy wilderness broken only by two young trees whose leaves were still green. But she did not care to see him. She sat on the end of the bench and leaned her head against the wood and spread her handkerchief over her eyes to keep out the sun. She would often sit like this, creating a closed circle of dimness for herself, feeling the cloth move up and down against her cheeks and eyelids, gently, with her breath. She called this "making a place"; wherever you went, you could always get a handkerchief, and then you could have a place. Under the handkerchief there was a warmth and a glow, and she was far away from *them* and from everything. Their voices, talking at the other end of the bench, seemed to be coming from a separate star.

"Concerning the giraffe," he was saying, "he's one of God's most witless creatures."

She sighed under the handkerchief. She was glad to have gotten that straight from the start; this giraffe was a he.

"Absolutely witless, and so mild that he probably wouldn't swallow a fly if it walked halfway down his tongue. He's herbivorous, you know. Eats green leaves—"

"And grass?" said the mother-voice, eager to get its two cents' worth of curious learning in.

"Not grass. No, indeed. Absolutely nothing off the ground." He was masculine and lordly now. "Look at him, and your common sense will tell you why."

"That silly neck? Too much trouble to get it down?"

"Trouble, my darling? Nothing so minor as trouble, I can assure you. A giraffe with his neck down is as good as a dead giraffe. He can't get it up again with any speed at all. That's why he's thirsty most of the time. He's afraid to drink. He goes for days without water, and you can imagine, in equatorial heat . . . "

She knew that word from her fourth-grade geography book. In the still place that she had made for herself, she imagined equatorial heat. There was a long, tan stretch of sandy earth, covered with smoky, weedy plumes. Here and there were little trees with a few fine leaves. For a while it was completely empty and still, and the giraffes came down. They came softly, gently, walking through weeds on their delicate feet. The great red sun burned upon them. All the lengths of their necks were dry with thirst, dry as sand. But they did not shove each other. They waited courteously, and each one had his small green spray and sucked the moisture out of it, as she had sucked a healing bitterness from the boxwood leaf.

"After a while, of course, the thirst gets to be too much for them.

They have to go down to the water hole. They go in droves, for moral support, I suppose, because, of course, they're utterly useless to each other. And then, when they've got their necks down and their tongues in the water, their backs are an invitation to whatever happens to be around. The tigers leap at them—"

And the black leopards, too, she thought.

She waited until her mouth stopped shaking and then took the handkerchief away from her face.

"Had a nice rest?" her mother said. "See, all you needed was a little quiet. And now, what are you going to do?"

"I think I'll go and look at the giraffe."

"Do, by all means."

She went slowly up to the cage, hoping that the giraffe would come close enough for her to see his eyes.

The place where the giraffe lived was more open than she had supposed. They knew he was a mild creature, and they had not closed him in too much. The room between the wire fence and the iron railing was only the length of her arm, and the diamonds of space between the crisscross wires were as big as her hand. Other children were standing close to the rail with their mothers and fathers, and nobody looked troubled or afraid. A dark Italian guard in a visored cap stood by, shaking his head at a little boy who looked as if he might throw a handful of peanuts between the wires.

It would have been better, she thought, if the guard had not been there. She recalled the time when, in a Philadelphia museum, just such a cap had borne down upon her because she had touched the toe of a kind, plump Virgin made of painted wood. She consoled herself with the thought that she had no peanuts or anything that could be mistaken for peanuts, and she leaned her elbows on the railing and stared into the giraffe's place, the quiet square of tan that had been made for him—in an alien country, to be sure, but at least away from black leopards and such. He was on the other side of the sandy stretch, beyond the fragile tree. She could not see him very well, and she amused herself with wondering whether he had to get his neck down often here. Maybe the people in charge of the zoo knew how hard it was for him to do that. Maybe they held his bucket up to him on a stick. And if they didn't, maybe they should be told in an anonymous letter, and then maybe they would.

While she was making up an anonymous letter, all the other

children drew in their breaths and said "Oh!" and she knew that the giraffe was coming from the other side of his place. She lifted her face and saw him, even taller than she had expected, his neck so long, his delicate nose held so high, that a person could imagine him nibbling at stars. He walked very slowly, with a graceful forward lurch. He made no clouds of dust with his little elegant feet. Now it seemed to her that she had never known anything about a giraffe before. She had thought he would be spotted, brown on beige. Instead, his colors were laid upon him in fine, soft squares. The closer he came, the more she delighted in this coloring. It was as if his hide had been made in two layers, one creamy and pale, the other crisp and reddish brown. Maybe the dark upper layer had been too fragile for the equatorial heat. It had cracked into blocks, like the glaze on the Chinese pottery she had seen at Mrs. Moss's house. It had cracked, and the tan under layer was foaming through. Such a soft belly too, that creamy tan; and, flashing past her, moist with a dream of plentiful springs, two great brown eyes. . . .

"Oh, my darling, oh, my beautiful," she said, holding the iron rail in her fists and pulling herself back and forth for pure joy.

It was as if he had heard her voice. He did not stay on the other side. He did not stop to sniff at the small tree. He made his swaying, processional way all round the inner side of the barrier of wire. She pressed hard against the rail. The other children, the guard, the two sitting on the bench behind her, the park, the whole world fell away. Her arms went up in a gesture of utter gratefulness. The giraffe had stopped just in front of her; he was looking at her; she was drowned in his sweet, wet glance. A warm brown well of sorrow and gentleness closed over her, and she was forever safe, everlastingly beloved.

"Oh, my sweet giraffe," she said, straining her body toward him across the railing, stretching the tips of her fingers to the highest wire she could hope to touch. Then she told him, not with her voice, only with her lips, that he was all the impossible things: all the friends from whom she had been taken, all the hands she had never touched, father and mother, unborn brother and sister, dear love, dear sad love.

There was an amazed chatter among the others around the railing. It was really remarkable, now wasn't it? The giraffe wanted to make friends with the little girl in the red jumper. Just look, he was stepping backward, he was getting his head down as far as he could, he was thrusting his soft, drooping nose into one of the spaces

174

between the wires. Even so, they could not quite meet, they could not quite touch. There were two inches of space between the tender nose and the raised hand.

"Do watch yourself, darling," a stout lady said. "You might lose a finger. You never can tell."

"Not him, not him," she chanted, swaying on her toes. "He's herbivorous, he never eats anything but leaves, and look at his eyes, he's good, he's kind."

He strove, and she strove with him, sensing the rasp of the wire against his nose. Her fingers trembled with the strain; pain ran around the socket of her shoulder like a ripple of fire.

Another breathless "Oh!" rose out of the throats of the watchers. The giraffe had found a way. He was bridging the empty space by thrusting out his tongue. It came out slowly, clean and moist and beautiful. It was a pale mauve color, and it turned silvery in the sunlight. It was warm. Its warmth and wetness advanced upon her, reached her, bestowed a long kiss on the center of her palm.

Then something shot across the wonder and the delight. She did not know at first what had come between her and her love; she knew only that the love was over, and that now she must feel what she had always felt at the end of any love—loneliness and shame. The dark hand that had shoved the giraffe's nose back was the guard's hand. The shadow of his visored cap was lying near her on cement.

"You mustn't do that, sister," the guard said.

She did not dare to look about her; there were so many staring eyes. She put her head down so far that her chin rested against the front of her jumper. "He wouldn't have bitten me," she said through the cottony mass of ache in her throat. "He was only licking my hand. He eats leaves. He doesn't bite."

"No, that's right. You're a smart girl. You know your animals, all right. He wouldn't hurt you, but you might hurt him."

I? Oh, no, how could that be, with so much love?

"You see, he's a very sensitive fellow. One little germ, and he's a goner. Now, I'm not saying your hands aren't clean. But you can't see germs. With germs, you never know."

They had risen and were coming up behind her. Her shoulders hunched against them. Their steps were soft upon the grass. And why was it so terrible? Why did she think that they had white, moonstone eyes?

"You must excuse her. Really, I thought she had better sense than that," her mother said.

She walked in front of them, away from the giraffe's home. She kept her hand closed in a fist. The moisture was still there; she still carried his kiss. All down the long path, longer because of the looks that were being turned upon her, she felt the wet glance trying to follow her. She wanted to turn to answer it, but her head was down. She had been to the deep brown pool and had swallowed her sweet drink. But now the time of drinking was over, and she could not raise her head.

"You certainly made an ass of yourself over that animal," said her father.

"But doesn't she always?" her mother said.

For weeks after that, she went about asking people questions about germs. She looked up the word in forbidding encyclopedias in unfamiliar libraries. She spent her candy money on the morning and evening papers and looked wildly up and down the columns, expecting every moment to see that the giraffe had died. Then one day she actually found an article about the giraffe. She saw his picture first and felt the cold squeeze of fear around her heart. But it was nothing; the giraffe was not dead; only he was a little unhappy because his keepers had not been able to find him a mate.

"I am your mate and your sister and your mother," she said to the picture, cutting it out with a borrowed pair of scissors in the art room at school. The teacher gave her a piece of red cardboard to paste it on and told her that it would make a beautiful bookmark. She pretended that it was a bookmark and kept it in her room in a story book.

But then they moved again, to a far city, and in the confusion the book was lost. Nothing was left but the remembrance of the silvery tongue brushing against her palm. Her mother coming in to see that she was well covered on the winter nights, wondered why she always fell asleep with her hand pushed hard against her lips.